Partnering with Nature

PARTNERING WITH NATURE

TRANSFORMATIVE ADVENTURES

MAUREEN SHEPARD

CELESTIAL GARDENS

Editing by Stephanie Gunning
Cover art and drawings by Z. Whitcombe
Interior design by Margaret Campbell
Back cover photo by Sheri Ross Fogerty

Celestial Gardens
P.O. Box 1713
Penn Valley, California 95946
www.Celestial-Gardens.com

ISBN 978-0-9911367-2-8

1. Spirituality 2. Memoir 3. Nature intelligence 4. Gaia
5. New age 6. Flower essences 7. Gardening

To Skidmore

CONTENTS

Prologue   The Magic Begins   1

Chapter 1   Let the Energy Come to Me   3

Chapter 2   The Mimzy Project   41

Chapter 3   The Domain of Love   67

Chapter 4   Mimzy Redux   89

Chapter 5   Sky Tour   101

Chapter 6   Essences of Flowers   121

Chapter 7   A Journey to Peru   153

Chapter 8   My True Home   171

Chapter 9   The Last Mimzy   201

Epilogue   The Magic Continues   229

Resources   230

Acknowledgments   233

Glossary   234

About Maureen Shepard   237

Join the Conversation   239

THE MAGIC BEGINS

My husband, Skidmore, is hiking in the lovely desert of Shamanic Valley in California. I'm sitting in our small RV, trying
to hold myself together as my world is rocked by a life-chang-
ing book: *Co-Creative Science* by Machaelle Small Wright. It's
a small trade paperback, copper- and gold-colored, and less
than 200 pages in length. It looks innocuous, but it shakes me
to the core.

Putting the book aside, I walk out into the desert, following
a raven that seems to be leading me forward as it moves ahead
in short, jumping flights. After a time, I stop walking and sit
in the shade of a small shrub to make my request. The raven
stops as well, landing close enough to me that I can see it
clearly.

It's one thing to read, think, and imagine. It's quite another
to act. Do I have the courage and resolution to commit to the
unknown? Do I have the skill, the time, and the resources to
live up to whatever will follow, or will I just fall on my face
and fail?

I feel small and alone. I take solace from the presence
of the raven. Am I imagining that this bird is offering me
support and companionship? I take a deep breath, summon

my deepest resolve, and say out loud to the Nature intelligence around me, "I want to be a student of Nature. Will you enroll me in your curriculum of co-creative science?"

I don't fully comprehend the implications of what I'm asking. I also don't really know if Nature has received my request. Am I delusional or have I actually communicated with an intelligence?

The raven cocks its head and appears to look at me a bit quizzically. Could it be that the raven is acting as an emissary of Nature, letting me know that I am being supported and accompanied on my quest?

After a time, I leave my shaded seat under the scrubby bush and return to the campground. The raven flies away into one of the palm trees that surround the oasis. I feel strange, yet I am hopeful that my life has now changed in some significant way.

They say the journey of a lifetime begins with one step. And all I had to do that October day was ask.

CHAPTER 1

LET THE ENERGY COME TO ME

In the days that follow my trip to Shamanic Valley, in the autumn of 2007, I return home and begin to create a life built upon the principles of working in partnership with Nature intelligence. As with most endeavors, I start by taking small steps, and build on my initial steps as I go. I create space in our home for an "office" for my work, and start a fall garden, using the processes given by Machaelle Small Wright in the *Perelandra Garden Workbook*.

The modest success of the garden is an encouraging sign that I might be on the right track. The larger success is the establishment of ongoing, almost daily connection sessions with aspects of Nature intelligence that I call my Nature team. We are getting to know one another and finding out what can be expected from each other. I'll be saying more about these connections and how they work later in this chapter.

We've all experienced a connection with the natural world. As you walk in a forest, feeling earth and pine needles below your feet, you have a kinesthetic experience of connection with the natural world. Maybe you sit on the forest floor, your back resting against an ancient tree, and sense the life processes of the tree taking place. The factory that is the tree is bringing water and nutrients up from the soil through its roots, and the leaves are exchanging gases with the air as they photosynthesize sunlight into energy. And maybe, in a transcendental moment, you actually perceive the tree and yourself as beings of light and energy, existing separately, but drawing sustenance from one source.

These moments of experiencing our connectedness to nature are profound and necessary to us and to our health as human beings. And yet our mystical connection with *nature* (denoted by a lower case *n*) does not create the partnership with *Nature* (meaning Nature intelligence denoted by an upper case N), which is the subject of this book. Partnership flows from intention, not experience alone.

When I first began working in partnership with Nature, I had no sense of actually connecting with anything. I certainly wasn't sure that I was communicating with an intelligence. Was I deluded? Was anyone actually there? I did know that I had intentionally asked for connection, so I proceeded as if the connection was real, just to see where that would take me. Where it took me was into a life more profoundly meaningful than I ever could have imagined. It took me on a journey, not just with Nature intelligence, but also into the depths of my own soul.

At first I imagined that my team could give me information that would allow me to plan my work out into the future. But I soon learned that they can only give me the next step. I can work with them to plan next season's garden on paper, but when I actually plant the garden changes might need to be made.

Here are some notes from my earliest garden sessions. I was asking Nature intelligence questions and the notes are my record of the answers.

November 9: Ants are herding aphids on the bok choy in the winter garden. Use Apis (a homeopathic remedy) on the bok choy to deal with the ants.

November 19: Decrease the watering time to 12 minutes a day. Put the compost pile on the north side of the garden outside the fence.

November 28: We can remove star thistle in January, February, or March by pulling it up or by burning it. Replace it with any legume in March or April. Don't plant grass. We can make a deer fence, but we'll need a dog as well.

December 3: I was rushing around preparing to leave, but I also wanted to check if anything was needed for the garden. I was asked to change the water to 14 minutes, which I did. Then I was asked to put cloth over the garden (presumably to make it warmer), but Skidmore didn't have time to make the frame. So I decided to tie the cloth over the garden as best I could. After doing that, I asked if there was anything else, and got a yes. I readjusted the cloth, asked if there was anything more needed, and still got a yes.

Finally I got the point, which was to center, slow down, connect, and have a grateful heart. I'm sure my rushing was difficult for the plants. Then I saw the plants waving in the breeze, a hawk circling above, and a woodpecker in a nearby tree, and I felt grounded. I decided to write this down in hopes of remembering it better.

Not exactly earth shattering, it was nonetheless useful information that I needed and could put to use directly. Later I would work with more esoteric energies, and the same principles continued to apply. If I asked the right questions, I received practical answers for immediate use.

How do I receive answers from Nature intelligence? Some people can hear the answers, but this doesn't happen for me. Some people can feel the answers by observing sensations within their entire bodies. They ask a question and feel the yes or no answer inside their bodies. They may find themselves swaying forward for yes and sideways for no, for instance. I don't usually receive answers in my body that way either. Other people use the swinging of pendulums to get their yes or no answers. Personally, I find using a pendulum too time consuming, so instead I use finger kinesiology as my primary tool for receiving answers. It's quick and easy, and can be done anywhere.

FROM THE PWN HANDBOOK

Kinesiology is a method for receiving answers to yes or no questions. Kinesiology, which is sometimes called *muscle testing,* is often used by a practitioner working with a patient. It's commonly used to determine which supplements will be beneficial to the patient. The patient holds a supplement in one hand while holding his or her other arm outstretched, parallel to the ground. The practitioner will then push down on the outstretched arm while telling the person to "resist." The person tries to hold his or her arm parallel while the practitioner tries to push it down.

The result of muscle testing can be surprising unless you're accustomed to it. When you are holding something that's not good for you, say some artificial sweetener, your arm will go weak, and it will not be possible to hold it up. If you're holding something that is good for you, your arm will remain strong and the practitioner will not be able to push it down.

The same process can be used to determine the answer to yes or no questions. If the answer is yes, the arm will remain strong. If the answer is no, the arm will go weak. Since this form of kinesiology takes two people and usually includes a trained practitioner, some people opt to use a pendulum instead.

Instead of using a pendulum, I taught myself finger kinesiology from instructions in Machaelle Small Wright's *Perelandra Garden Workbook* so that I could receive answers quickly and easily without the help of a second person. It works because energetically we all register the rightness or wrongness of things physically, and our bodies react in a way that's outside our conscious control.

If you're interested in learning finger kinesiology, watch one of the many helpful videos on the topic that are available online. They can be found easily by searching the term "self-kinesiology video." My favorite one is from the Perelandra Center for Nature Research and can be found by searching "Perelandra Kinesiology Testing Technique."

If you are one of the few people who can "hear" the answer to a question posed to Nature intelligence with your inner hearing, you won't need kinesiology to receive yes or no answers.

A SATISFYING CROSSING

As Nature intelligence and I continue our work together, I find that I need to ask fewer questions. I can distinguish more answers in my gut, rather than having to ask yes or no questions and use finger kinesiology. I also learn to ask for a "download" of information on a subject so that I can receive relevant information without having to ask specific questions. A *download* is information received from beyond our senses, often bypassing our conscious understanding. I don't grasp the content of the information as the download is happening. But later, when the time comes for action, I find that I know what to do.

Once I can use finger kinesiology, I begin to use flower essences, both for energy work on others and to balance my own energy. A *flower essence* is a solution created by floating flower petals on water in the sun, releasing an energetic healing pattern into the water. Years before I had used a flower essence that was prescribed for me and had enjoyed the sense of calmness and contentment that I experienced as a result. Now I learn to test essences for myself and to take orally the ones that test positive.

I learn this just in time to help my 91-year-old father, who has moved from an independent living facility to my sister's home and is under hospice care. My mom, his wife of 53 years, has passed on several years before.

Having learned that any activity can be enhanced by balancing the soil that supports that activity, I work with Nature to balance the soil and cleanse the energy of my sister Sue's land with the special intention that my dad be supported in his death process. I also test essences for him using kinesiology and make a solution of the essences he needs.

The next day, I repeat this process, with special attention to balancing the soil beneath the room where my dad is staying, again intending that he be able to move easily through the death process.

That night I wake at 2:55 a.m. knowing that my dad has passed. Within five minutes the phone rings, and before answering I already know that it is Sue calling. After speaking to her briefly, I move to my office, sitting at my desk with my flower essences to do a post-death essence process. This process involves using flower essences to balance and stabilize the person who has passed.

I carefully follow the steps of the process, opening a Nature connection, connecting to the higher self of my dad, and asking him if he would like to receive flower essences. I use kinesiology to receive his answer. He confirms that he understands about flower essences, he remembers taking them before, and he'd like them now. So I test essences and shift the ones he needs to him via a Nature spirit connection. I'll say more about how this connection works later.

The process allows me to talk to my dad for a half hour before saying goodbye and closing the connection. I thank him for being my father and raising me, and I tell him I love him. After a couple of minutes of this, I get a distinct impression of impatience from him, almost as if he is checking his watch. I'm amused. He's so well-balanced now that he wants to get on with it. He has places to go and people to see. I say goodbye and close the connection, filled with happiness that I've been able to assist him in his crossing over.

I'm thrilled that in less than three months of living a partnering with Nature lifestyle, I've learned enough to help another person in such a profound way. Sometimes I've wondered if I'm imagining all this. But the connection with my dad is so authentic, so clearly a connection with the man I knew, that my doubts recede and I become even more committed to my new way of life.

FROM THE PWN HANDBOOK

When we think of nature, we think of trees, mountains, sea, and the great outdoors. But these are just one aspect of nature. Nature is defined as the order, organization, and life vitality of all form. Form is anything we can interact with through our senses, or through our extrasensory perception. Nature has an intelligence that we can connect with, even though this intelligence is not centered in a brain and a sensory system.

Humanity and Nature each has its own specialty. Humanity's specialty is soul evolution through exercise of free will. Nature's specialty is balance. The human reality always contains free will, and Nature's reality always contains inherent balance.

Our planet is out of balance because of the actions of humans. By understanding and partnering with Nature, we can make decisions that will rebalance our planet. When we use only our free will to solve our problems it's like trying to ride a bicycle without using our sense of balance. It won't work, and we only end up falling.

For us as humans, one of the first steps to understanding co-creative partnership with Nature is to learn more about how our intentions create form. It is the soul that creates intention, but intention is only part of creation. The soul alone cannot bring an intention into form. That is the job of Nature. Nature intelligence is the ruler of form. It's our job to set our intentions. It's Nature's job to provide the means to bring our intentions into form, actualizing them in the physical world.

These two domains, the domain of soul and the domain of Nature, together create our bodies and the world. It's good to know that if we, as a global people, desire and intend some change anywhere on our planet, Nature will get busy providing us with the material tools needed to make that happen.

We too frequently ignore our partner in creation, and then we wonder why things don't work well. Our disregard of Nature brings us endless misery, but we persist in thinking that somehow we can dominate our magnificent partner.

People often say, "I just love nature." But Nature doesn't care if we love it or not. Nature's domain is not the domain of feeling. That belongs to us. What Nature wants is our agreement to work in co-creative partnership with it in accordance with the grand design for our universe.

The Right Place for Us

Early in 2008, I become aware that Skidmore and I are approaching a major decision. Our two acres is too small for all we would like to do, and we are considering buying land in the region and renting out the house we're living in. In mid-January we meet with a realtor to tour possible properties.

Among other things, I realize the property we are seeking must be conducive to my work with Nature. This will be land that we will care for and improve in partnership with Nature. In my mind, the land will be "ours," meaning that it will belong to my husband, me, and Nature. The land will provide us with a more extensive campus for our School of Nature and the unfolding of Nature's curriculum.

Choosing the property will be the first important decision I will make in partnership with Nature. For the first day of land viewing I don't want to stay connected to my Nature team all day, because it can be tiring. So I ask if some sort of map of what we are looking for can be transmitted to me, so that I can access the needed information without having to keep a session open. I have an amazing sensation as this apparently takes place. I definitely feel as though some sort of "information module" has been downloaded into my sensory system.

On the first day of viewing, Skidmore and I learn that we are unclear about exactly what we're looking for, and that each of us is giving priority to different attributes. We soon make a list of what each of us wants and doesn't want. From this list, we compile a list of features we must have and aspects we need to avoid. I double check each item on the list with Nature to be sure it adequately reflects what is needed. I want to continue gardening, so room for gardens and fruit trees becomes one of our requirements.

The power of writing down what you want is amply demonstrated by what happens next. We later learn that the day after we make the list, our destined home and acreage is put on the market. A week later, on a gray rainy day, we see it for the first time. It's a pathetic looking place. There is junk strewn about outside, rusting or rotting away. In the house, there is a leak in a corner with a bucket catching the drip. But other than needing a new roof, the house is sound. The view across a small valley to the hills beyond is inspiring even on such a dreary day.

More importantly to me, I think I sense joy from the Nature spirits of the land.

I leave my husband and the realtor, and walk down to a firebreak road and into the undeveloped part of the land. This is the area where nature holds sway. Here there are dramatic outcroppings of rocks, some covered with moss. There are manzanita trees, buckbrush, and toyon with their holly-shaped leaves and red berries.

I stand among the dripping trees and bushes, open a connection to Nature, and try to sense if this is the place we are to do our work together. This decision is too important to use kinesiology to find the answer. When so much is riding on an answer, you can't be sure of the result. You may be unconsciously influencing the answer without realizing it. I have to rely on my gut feeling, and that of my husband, to know if this is the right place for us.

Over the next few days, the feeling that this is our right place grows within me. My husband is happy visualizing improvements he can make. I know now that I was probably processing this decision in my dreams. We negotiate an offer to buy and five weeks later move into our new home.

Over the next few years, we make many of the changes to the land and house that we originally visualized. We create organic gardens and a small orchard. My husband puts in wood floors and enlarges my office. As we envisioned, we now keep chickens and have a dog. All of these were created as projects in partnership with Nature, and as part of my curriculum in the School of Nature.

The First Grounding Stake

Even though homeopathy is over 200 years old, it is a medicine that will be used more widely in the future when its principles will be more easily grasped. In the spring of 2008, I had a hazy understanding that information can be seated within the Earth, making it more accessible to seekers. I'll say more about how the Earth holds information later in this book.

I go with friends on a hike to Codfish Falls in the Sierra Nevada foothills of Northern California. It's a beautiful day, sunny and warm. Arriving at the falls, I stand in the mist wafting from the falling water. I don't feel as though I'm alone. It's as if some presence is nudging me, trying to get my attention. I open a connection to Nature. "Is there something I am to do here?" I ask. I'm told that I can ground homeopathy more firmly on the planet by placing a grounding stake here.

What? I can do that? I have some experience with moving energy through visualization. I open myself to being a conduit for the energy. I visualize a tall, thin, brightly shining stake grounding homeopathy. The stake moves diagonally downward and finally anchors into the ground right in front of the falls. I realize that my deep desire for homeopathy to be more firmly grounded on the planet, plus my openness to working with Nature, has allowed my partners to employ me as the human intermediary for this work.

THE SECOND GROUNDING STAKE, SPRING EQUINOX, 2008

Today Nature and I place a second grounding stake for homeopathy in the Canyon of the Ravens' Nests, which is not far from the Shamanic Valley campground. The moment of the equinox occurs at 9:48 a.m., and we place the stake around 11:00 a.m., using the same procedure as we did with the first stake. The ravens' nests are built high on the cliffs above us.

Immediately after planting the stake, my hiking companions and I see a raven pair bring a piece of paper towel to the highest nest. One raven stands in front of the nest, cawing at us, while the other carefully arranges the paper towel.

My friends are surprised that the ravens would come to

the nest while we are there, and they interpret the cawing as warning us off. To me the cawing feels like a celebration of the energy present.

A few minutes later, as we're hiking away, we see a red-tailed hawk pair flying low above us and across our path. One of the pair is carrying a bunch of soft vegetation, presumably for their nest.

EASTER SUNDAY, 2008

I notice in the *Perelandra Garden Workbook* that all the energy processes include balancing and stabilizing afterward. I regret that I did not do balancing and stabilizing after planting the second stake, so I walk to an area near a labyrinth above the campground where there is a panoramic view of the mountains. I open a connection and ask if balancing and stabilizing should be done now, even though it is three days later. I receive a no.

I ask if the stake is still there, and if it is well-planted. I receive a yes, but I also "see" (in my inner vision, I think), the upper part of the huge stake angling down behind the mountain. It looks somewhat like a jet stream trail.

Just then, a small plane takes off from the airstrip below. It rises, circles around, does acrobatic loops, and comes by me low and fairly close. I wave. It circles around again, flies back, and tips its wings to me. I laugh in amazement and delight. This joyous feeling is like a gift from Nature, letting me know that my team is celebrating with me. For the first time, I'm full-out laughing with my team. I feel that they are signaling me not to worry—I'm doing just fine.

MAKING THE "JUNE DAY" REMEDY, JUNE 7, 2008

In reference to a problem with a rodent in the vegetable garden, I'm guided to gather some pollen and dried buds from local plants growing nearby. I use the materials to make a homeopathic remedy. I crush the dry materials with a mortar and pestle then put them through a fine sieve. I mix one milliliter of this powder with 99 parts brandy/water mixture (60 percent 80-proof brandy and 40 percent purified water). I succuss this mixture 40 times to get a 1C potency. Each succussion is a firm "thump" of the vial on a thick book. I repeat the dilution and succussion steps 11 more times to get a 12C potency. I name the remedy "June Day" after the lovely day on which it was made.

I apply the remedy to the plants in the vegetable garden five times in June, July, and August. The application of the June Day remedy appears to have strongly ameliorated the damage done to the garden by the rodent. Several people tell me that the garden plants will continue to be pulled underground until none are left. This did not happen. We lost a few vegetables, but otherwise the plants thrived and produced.

Some say that for every malady there is a cure nearby in the local vegetation. The making of this remedy and my success with it makes me think that this may be true.

WIND: JOURNAL ENTRY, OCTOBER 28, 2008, SHAMANIC VALLEY CAMPGROUND

Wind. Rocking my small RV like a boat on the water. Stinging my eyes as I walk into it. Strewing sand across the landscape. Pushing me from behind, propelling my journey back from the outhouse. There is a resistance inside of me that fights against the wind, tiring me out. I sit warm and protected inside the RV while my friends are out hiking in the wind. I don't envy them. I'm enjoying this quiet space, this island of solitude in the sea of sociability here at the campground.

The wind at this campground may blow for days without stopping—just increasing and then decreasing for a bit, then speeding up again, making desert tree limbs flail and tent fabric flap. But when it stops, it suddenly disappears. From one moment to the next, it's suddenly and completely gone. Like this wind, the winds of change are blowing, buffeting all of us around. Some people adjust to it, and others resist, trying somehow to deflect it away.

A raven has just landed nearby and I see that his landing is a bit jagged because he has to hop a bit to recover. In my at-home life, I'm always hurried and a bit jagged as I'm trying to adjust to this wind of change that has continuously sped up to the point that almost everyone now feels it. It is an entity now, something almost tangible, the elephant in the room that only a few of us talk about, but we all know it's there. When it has done its work, when it's no longer needed, will it just suddenly disappear like the wind in the desert?

Post-election Process: November 5, 2008

This is the day after the election of Barack Obama to be the U.S. president. The country is divided into partisan camps with harsh feelings on both sides. I am guided to do a ceremony of healing. I feel out of my comfort zone. How can one person affect this dynamic? Am I delusional even to be attempting it?

Yet I trust my team, and feel that I am being asked to do

this, so I decide to do what I can. I walk to the labyrinth on higher ground above the Shamanic Valley Campground.

I open a session with my Nature spirit team. As I'm walking the labyrinth, a private plane comes over and circles several times, similar to the occurrence the previous spring on Easter Sunday. The need to add three more team members to the connection is conveyed to me. The scope of the three entities intimidates me, but I connect to them anyway: the Overlighting Deva of the United States, the Overlighting Deva of American Politics, and the Overlighting Deva of Human Evolution.

I balance myself with flower essences and then begin the Perelandra energy cleansing process. The area to be cleansed is the entire United States. I complete all the steps of the process, working as slowly and carefully as I can. Then I perform the Perelandra battle energy release process. Then I walk the labyrinth again.

Five months later, I am asked to repeat both processes. Since I can't travel to Shamanic Valley, I perform them from my office at home, but I imagine myself to be at the labyrinth and I energetically execute them as if from there.

Waiting in Readiness: Journal Entry,
October 24, 2009, Shamanic Valley Campground

Before the party quiet. Everything pauses in readiness. I thought I heard a drum, but perhaps it's just the drumbeat of things to come. Tonight's drumming echoing back into the heat of today's afternoon. As I look up from my writing, a coyote runs across my field of vision, maybe 30 feet away. Will he circle back to the water cache and drink there?

Maybe I'll hear him howling with his companions as I did in the wee hours of this day's morning. Coyote, raven, grackle, and me—all pulsating, vibrating with the same life, all pausing expectantly, all waiting for the twist of energy, the sleight of hand that will shift us into a new era of life on our beautiful planet.

COYOTE REVERIE

We saw a coyote today, my dog Skip and I, standing at the top of the ridge, silhouetted against the dawning sky. The three of us paused and looked at each other. These two cousins, one wild, the other leashed to his human companion, each caught a glimpse of the other's life. Some would say that the free primitive life of the coyote is a better life than the life of the domesticated dog. But all life is sacred; all is pulsating with the energy and consciousness that enlivens even the rocks.

The song of the coyote, the song of the dog, and the song of me are melodies that long to harmonize with the cosmic symphony. May the songs of the coyote, dog, and woman blend harmoniously with the songs of this day and this place, and with the songs of all the beings that are here at the beautiful and mysterious Shamanic Valley Campground.

COYOTES AGAIN

Long shadows. The sage bushes are only eight inches tall, yet they cast five-foot shadows in the slanted sunlight. October morning, the sun has barely crested the mountain and the campground is still. The ravens cast long shadows too as they hop comically over the sand near the desert labyrinth. Later

I will walk the labyrinth, holding a wish for happiness for all. For now I just walk with Skip and gaze at the splendor of the mountains.

A jolt of surprise: There are two coyotes 30 feet away. How did they come to be so close in this flat desert area without us seeing them sooner? Were the mountains so gorgeous and the ravens so mesmerizing that we failed to see the approach of two coyotes? Or did they just appear, transported here from another mysterious dimension in time or space?

How little we really know of our life on this planet and how it all works. We think we understand coyotes, but we do not. We don't even understand our dogs or our own selves. We don't understand dark energy, the music of the spheres, who the extraterrestrials are, or why we're experiencing a massive shift of consciousness at this time. The unity of gravity, electromagnetism, and the weak and strong nuclear forces is still to be explained. And somewhere in the explanation of the unknown is a footnote that explains beautiful, powerful, dynamic homeopathy, the art and science that is so special to me, the science of healing that I love.

Later: This time I heard them first. Lapping water behind me in the rosy light as the sun drops behind the opposite mountain. I turn around and there are five coyotes drinking from the overflow of the water cache. This time I am the one who is watching, unseen by them.

IN THE CANYON OF THE RAVENS' NESTS

A long, thin, wispy cloud angles down behind the mountain, tracing the trajectory of an anchor I helped ground one and a half years ago. There is a *ley line*, or planetary meridian, there and the anchor is making the art and science of homeopathy more available to all of us on the planet. The ravens know the ley line is there. They build their nests in the cliffs above it, just as humans built sacred sites on ley lines in ancient times. If you sit on one of the huge boulders in the canyon and become still, then look slowly and carefully, you can see their nests above you on the cliff walls.

Close your eyes and you may sense the power of the ley line. If you know it's there, or if you believe it's there because I have told you, you may be able to trace the straight line of the anchor as it angles down from above the crest of the mountain to its grounding site on the canyon floor.

Making homeopathy more stable, grounding it—why was I chosen for this work? Because I love homeopathy. Because I believe we need this medicine and the other energetic medicines, especially at this time. Because I can work with other intelligences and make myself available to be the human assistant in this kind of project. Because I love structure and grounding, so the intention of grounding an anchor into the structure of the ley lines can be transmitted through me. Because I was the right person at the right time and unfolding energy chose me.

OUTDOOR SHOWER, SHAMANIC VALLEY CAMPGROUND

Outdoor shower in the palms. I put my bag of toiletries on the hide-covered stool and pull out tiny bottles of shampoo and conditioner. I don't bother with soap because someone has left a huge box of soap bars on the nearby glass tabletop, free for the taking. Several partly used bars are close by, resting inside the open yellow mouth of a green ceramic frog.

I pull down on the lever for hot water and carefully climb into the tub. A rush of enjoyment suffuses through me as the water hits my body. I pull down on the cold water lever until the temperature is perfect. Through the palm trees I can see the massive shapes of the mountains. I take a sliver of the oatmeal soap I've been using all week and wash my face. Then I shampoo my hair, massaging my scalp vigorously. The water on my back keeps me warm despite the soft breezes gently eddying around my wet body. Then the glorious rinse, the water cascading off my crown and streaming down over all of me.

I use plenty of conditioner to moisturize my hair in this dry climate. Then I take the wet sliver of oatmeal soap and rub it all over my body, watching as it leaves tracks of tiny bubbles on my arms and legs. A final joyous rinse, the water rushing over me one last time. I watch the water and tiny soap bubbles swirl around and down the drain.

Later I will walk across the lawn to the pond where this water empties. I'll cross the small bridge there and see the orange and white speckled goldfish darting away as I pass by. But for now I just feel grateful to be here in this enchanting shower.

PORTRAIT OF MY EIGHT-YEAR-OLD SELF: JOURNAL ENTRY, DECEMBER 2, 2009

I'm a short girl with short, blond hair and bangs. I wear a plaid dress with a sash tied in a bow in the back. I wear socks and shoes tied with laces and a jacket to keep me warm on my walk to school on this chilly autumn day. I like some of the playground games: jump rope, hopscotch, and jacks. I play with the others. Some are girls from my scout troop, Joan and Leah and Patty. I like school okay, but mostly I like books.

Storybooks take me to other worlds and into the lives of other people, some far away. My family prefers watching TV. My mom urges me to watch TV with the rest of the family, to be more sociable. But TV is boring. It doesn't grab my imagination and hold me entranced, almost breathless to find out what happens next the way that books do. The pretend life in a book seems more interesting—and easier—than my real life. I don't really have much in common with my mom, my dad, or my sister. My baby sister is too young; I don't realize that we will be connected later.

Mom is the most important person in my life. I admire her, I like her sometimes, and I love her as my mom. She's an atheist and I'm spiritual, so we don't understand each other. I figure that since I'm just a kid, my mom must be right, and maybe someday I'll understand why. The spiritual yearnings inside me can't be talked about or even acknowledged by those around me. I think that I must be wrongly focused somehow. And I don't know what to do about it. But I do know what I refuse to do. I won't pretend to like TV if I don't. I won't try to be pretty and popular if I really have no desire for it. I won't fake it. Otherwise I might lose myself and not know who I really am anymore. I feel I must somehow keep track of myself and hold on to my shaky awareness of who I genuinely am. Hold on until what? I don't know. Just keep holding on until I can get some kind of support, some kind of validation, or some way of finding a wider roomier space for myself.

If my eight-year-old self could see my current self, she would feel pure relief in the realization that I wasn't wrong. I was just isolated. Thank God there was a way to move beyond the narrowness of my eight-year-old situation. I fought for it! And I found it! My determination did not forsake me.

And now I can even help other people in their journeys! How incredibly wonderful that is. It's a gift that I never imagined I would receive. There's nothing that my eight-year-old self wouldn't like about my life now. It's a richer and happier and more blessed life than she could conceive of in all of her yearnings. I feel so much love for her because she was a real trooper and never let me down. She walked in constant self-doubt, but she never gave up. Her heroism inspires me as I walk into the unknown future. Her spirit within me can be a refuge in times of trouble. A voice within me saying, *I won't give up. I won't fake it. I will be myself. I will take my chances that who I really am will be good enough.*

From the PWN Handbook

Let's assume that I'm planning to do a shared project in partnership with Nature. How do I go about it?

First I specify in writing what the goal of the project is. Do I want to write a book, plant a garden, open a retail store, build a birdhouse, or just rearrange my furniture? I don't specify too many details about the outcome. I want to leave room for our partnership to actualize something even better than what I can visualize.

I write down significant limitations, such as "I can only devote two hours a day to our project" or "I must be able to be run my business from my home."

I also write down the underlying reasons I'm doing the project. Do I want the furniture rearranged because I'm bored with the old arrangement? Or do I want to fit a new piece of furniture into my home? Am I planting a vegetable garden to save money on food costs? Or do I want homegrown produce because it's fresher and tastes better?

You may remember that I stated that Nature unfolds manifestation from our intention. This is an automatic process, which happens whether or not we're conscious of it. People are in a relationship with nature one way or the other. So why bother initiating a formal project with Nature intelligence? Why do I bother to write down my goals and purpose if it's going to happen anyway?

It's important to know that formally creating a project expands the power of your intention exponentially. The clearer your intention, the better Nature can form the means to realize it. That doesn't mean that you sit by and wait for it to happen. You must be willing to do whatever action is required. The combination of clear intention followed by action in cooperation with Nature creates a shift in the field of possibilities through which change can manifest.

Once I've progressed this far, Nature will begin creating form for my project, whether or not I am consciously aware of it. Nature will create a blueprint or archetype for the project. The part of Nature intelligence that creates the blueprint is sometimes called the *devic level* and the blueprint itself is sometimes called a *deva*. I can easily connect with this deva by just asking to be connected. For example, if my project is called the Fantastic Furniture Formation Project, known as the 3F Project for short, I can say, "I'd like to be connected to the Deva of the 3F Project," and I will automatically be connected.

Besides connecting with the deva of my project, I normally connect with additional entities according to the steps given by Machaelle Small Wright in the *Perelandra Garden Workbook*.

Since Nature intelligence is so vast and multilayered, it works well to connect with a universal aspect of Nature known as Pan. This aspect has been visualized as a man or a goat, although it is neither. I visualize Pan as a masculine being, so I will continue the ancient tradition of referring to "him" as such in this book.

Another connection that I make is with a group that has been known from ancient times as the Great White Brotherhood. *White* denotes the light, and *Brotherhood* denotes a community of humans standing in solidarity for the cause of human evolution on this planet. Their current work involves forwarding the ongoing planetary transition that we are presently experiencing. When you connect with them, you can more easily align your project with the ongoing direction of planetary development. Even a new furniture arrangement will be more pleasing if it energetically "fits" with the unfolding planetary energies. I ask to be connected to the appropriate White Brotherhood members for working on my project.

I also connect to my higher self. I think of my higher self as the part of me that is eternal and exists outside of space and time.

Once I'm connected to the deva of my project and the other entities, then what?

Then I can start holding meetings with this team, asking questions and using kinesiology to get yes or no answers. I ask questions about any issues I'm facing regarding my project. I keep written notes of the decisions made at each meeting. I've found my notes to be a valuable asset to refresh my memory over time. Also, when reviewing them later, I find patterns and perspectives that I didn't fully perceive at the time. After looking back over a period of some years, I can see how elegantly my team has tailored their responses to my understanding and capacity at the time.

When finished with the meeting, I close the connection in reverse order. It's important to close the connection as soon as the meeting is over, because the connection is tiring to the mind and body. Otherwise, I'll feel drained.

I continue to meet with the team regularly, and especially any time a major decision must be made. The connection can happen anywhere. I often connect while shopping for supplies for my projects, because it turns out that my team is pretty particular about which tools and supplies are used. I silently ask my team questions, in my mind. Other shoppers around me don't seem to notice that I'm using my fingers to test products, and naturally they're not aware of the connection.

On rare occasions, someone looks at me and does a double take. I assume that this person can see the connection. I myself wouldn't normally know what the connection looks like, because I can't see it. It was described to me once by a clairvoyant who could see it. She described it as a vortex of light at the height of my head and to my left. Later it was caught in a photo and looked just as she had described. Should you decide to try this, your connection may look completely different. We're all individuals so there's sure to be lots of variation.

Exercise: Create a Low-risk Project

The best way to begin connecting to Nature intelligence is to identify a small project you'd like to accomplish that doesn't need to be done perfectly, a project that you can mess up and it's still okay. That way, if Nature gives you answers that seem unconventional or even wacky, you can try them anyway just to see what happens.

Give your project a name and write down what the goals of the project are. Identify in writing any significant limitations.

You can now connect to the deva of your project and other entities if you so choose. Once connected, ask yes or no questions about your project and how Nature recommends that you proceed. Just ask a few questions in the first session, because the connection can be tiring, especially in the beginning. Record the answers to your questions.

When you're ready to close the session, disconnect from each entity in the opposite order from which you made the connections.

Now you're ready to do the most consequential part of this exercise. It's important to take some action on your project that is based on the information you received. Creating a project and asking your team questions really doesn't do much. When you take action, you affect the field of possibility, drawing more desirable outcomes toward you.

NEW FRIENDS

After some months of working on our new home and its gardens, I start to make friends in the area. I'm invited to join a women's group that's forming, and there I meet Wendy, Sybil, and Denna, all women who will play a part in my later story. Denna is a professional writer, and soon I join her writing class along with Sybil and Sybil's friend Ursa. I don't think of myself as a writer. However, Ursa is a psychic and she encourages me, telling me that I will be a writer in the future.

It is at the writing class, as people are arriving and chatting before the class starts, that I overhear Ursa and Sybil talking about something they're calling the Mimzy Project. Each time they mention it, it captures my attention and I feel a strong pull toward whatever it is. The third time I overhear them, I look at them and say, "When you talk about that, you're hooking me."

Ursa looks at me and replies, "That's because you're supposed to be part of it."

I already realize that I'm supposed to be part of it. So even though I've only been told that the project involves some mysterious "beings," and even though I don't resonate with that explanation at all, I sign up to participate in the project scheduled for around Easter 2010.

Toward the end of 2009, I decide to throw a big birthday party for myself in honor of my 60th birthday. I engage a band for live music and dancing, and a caterer to prepare a barbecue dinner. Since the party will be held during the holidays, I invite 100 people, hoping that at least 60 will be able to make it. It ends up being an upbeat, fun party with a great band and good food. About 65 people attend, including new friends, old friends, relatives, and clients. I'm so proud of myself for believing in myself enough to make this public statement that my life is worth celebrating.

Early the next year, as I continue with the writing class, I experience a phenomenon that is new to me. In the middle of writing, I start to receive images that appear to be coming from my Nature team. I translate the images into words as best I can. Since I'm seemingly not the source of the information, the words come through as though the team members are directly speaking to me, or to a group of us. In the journal entries that follow, you'll sometimes notice the point of view of the speaker shifts in this way. When this happens, it's because I've stopped writing from my own viewpoint and started to record the information as I'm receiving it.

The first time this happened, I was taken completely by surprise. I hadn't realized that this could happen to me or that I could respond to it by writing down the words. Denna, our writing teacher, began the class by playing a piece of symphonic music and asking us to write to it. I started writing from my point of view, but later the shift occurs.

MANIFESTATION SYMPHONY

Drops of essence are dropping from another place of being onto our plane, where we can see them. Pan is playing the piano. The notes are like the notes of his flute, each one vibrating a receptor in my spine. These are the notes of creation, moving energy into form that we can see and touch. As he plays, energy coalesces into the things of our world. I watch as he and his assistants move the energy, slowly, slowly, ever so slowly. With each small motion, the energy becomes slightly denser. It's unfolding, slowly unfolding into being on our planet. So beautiful. I can see flowers, trees, minerals, and animals coalescing into being. Among them are the beings I work with: the substances of homeopathy.

The petals of *Bryonia alba*—he doesn't want to move, leave him alone. The petals of *Pulsatilla nigricans*—she wants her mother. The mineral *Silica*—my personal benefactor and enricher of the soil. *Arsenicum*—I can help you when you feel like you're dying. A hummingbird flies from one flower to another, pollinating as she goes. Pan brings forth more flowers to support her. Many, many more exist in the ether. Pan with his music is bringing them slowly to us, the violins helping, as they become denser, until we can see them with the eyes of our body. Finally they're all the way here, present now with us here on this gorgeous planet.

Let's spend a moment just listening to the music and appreciating this miracle of creation, this ongoing process that never ceases. All we want to do is align ourselves with this energy, to find some way to be a creative part of the unfolding. To share it with others so they can see how precious all life is on this planet, and how much care and energy is being lavished on us so that we and the plants, animals, and minerals can be here and have this experience. We are so blessed. We can choose to celebrate our life here whenever we wish to remember this or whenever we fall into this music and let it take us to the place where Pan plays beings into creation.

> *We the Nature spirits send you our love and an invitation to be in partnership with us. Together we can do great things. This is the way your planet was designed: as a partnership between humans and Nature. We each have our own realm and our own work. Be in partnership with us and we can open the door to the most amazing love and beauty your world has seen. This is the plan. This is what we as Nature and you as humanity are called to do. We can only invite and wait in patience for your answer. As humans you have free will and choice. So we wait. When you are ready, we will be there. Our yearning speaks to your yearning. Bring this message to others. If they feel the yearning, they will join us in co-equal partnership.*

GRATITUDE: JOURNAL ENTRY, JANUARY 20, 2010

Today I am grateful for gratitude itself, and for the ability to feel this most angelic emotion. I see certain clients who cannot at first feel gratitude. Every unwanted circumstance happens to them, everything difficult is done to them, and that's why they think they are in the dark night of the soul. Their pain, their suffering draws my compassion. I wish that I could shift their perspective. Just a tiny twist in the way they look at life and everything changes. It's not about them, the state of their finances, whether someone loves them, or whether their loved one has died. It's about what they have to give. This tiny shift in perspective, what a difference it makes!

I'm grateful for my expanding heart. All my intelligence and abilities are nothing against the chaos of the world. In my heart I take my stand and nothing can move me. The source of love, dimly perceived, is my anchor. When I connect with it my heart opens further. I feel it entering the front of my heart as a slender beam of light. It exits from the back of my heart like spreading wings. Then my eyes close and the single eye that abides opens.

The transience of the world falls away and I am one with eternity. The galaxies can spin, the suns can go nova, but eternal truth never changes. I thank the source of all that I can feel this and that I know it's real and that all my yearning only comes back to the source of love.

We all dance the dance of duality. Light will come and the shadow. Pleasure and pain. Chaos certainly, becoming stronger at this time of earth change. We take our roles, the ones we've chosen, the assignments we've accepted. It's all good, all part of the plan. On this planet there are those who think life is about what they can take for themselves. In another time/place reality, they are the ones who bring love and comfort to others. I want to see an image of their human greed superimposed with an image of their human love. Two images: Neither one is good or bad, neither one is best.

I'm grateful that I can come to the still place within where all are loved, where none is best. This still place is where I want to spend some time every day, opening myself to the source, basking in the light, and receiving its sometimes demanding guidance. I am grateful for the guidance, because it shows me that I have work to do and a useful role to play, and I am honored. I'm grateful that I've been given tasks that are big, and I'm grateful for the trust to know that they're not too big.

> *You are loved now and forever. All the suns in the universe are but floating candles burning in an ocean of limitless love. The spark of love burns in you now and forever.*

Starting School: Journal Entry, February 3, 2010

Four beginnings: starting university, starting yoga school, starting homeopathy school, and starting in the School of Nature. These beginnings were like fractal images of each other, each one a landing in the spiral stairway of my life that allowed me to access what would be needed for the next stage of growth. I loved every second of learning in each of the four schools. I breathed in the teachings and let them saturate my body with joy. Each one was an initiation.

When I went to the university I attended, I was just 17 and alone in my new city of Houston, where I knew not one person. This was a time for basics, such as how to be on my own, make all my own decisions, and provide for my own food, living space, and transportation. How I loved being free to do things my way! I learned to create a life by making choices. You would have to have lived an overly controlled childhood to know how good that feels.

What led up to it? I earned the grades, I took the SATs twice, and I applied for, and won, a scholarship through the grace of God plus hard work.

My second school, a summer of yoga classes at Ananda Village, gave me the guidance I was yearning for. Loving God is the joy of my life, but I was burdened with what little outdated theology I'd been able to assemble. What relief to be given useful teaching and techniques that allowed me to pursue a spiritual life with coherence and meaning!

What led up to it? I had met a yogi who came to Houston about once a year. It was up to me to discern that his teachings provided me with an opportunity, a doorway. I got the money for the class, I got my then-husband's support, I got myself to Ananda Village, and I showed up for the class.

Homeopathy school, how I loved every second of it. It was as if I couldn't get enough, couldn't breathe in or fill myself full enough. I still wanted more. Even today, after the infatuation of those days has passed, the depth of homeopathy draws me powerfully, and I continue to absorb more, master more. Homeopathy school changed me in many ways, but one way in particular: It opened my intuition. Because it's an art and a science, it demands that you use both the right brain and the left brain. And I loved it enough to open myself to intuition despite all the warnings of my mother and the probable derision of cynics everywhere.

What led me to study homeopathy? This one caught me by surprise, because I wasn't consciously looking for it. I was 52 years old and had earned the possibility of retiring at 55. My son Dickon was living with his father and stepmother. My son Thor was still in high school, living with me. My then-fiancé, Skidmore, said, "If you could do anything you wanted to do, what would it be?"

At that moment, I truthfully said what was in my heart, even though it seemed too big and unrealistic. I said, "I'd like to be a homeopath."

He said, "Let's see how you can do that." I chose the right husband!

And now I am enrolled in the latest, ongoing school of working with Nature spirits and the White Brotherhood. This is a most generous and demanding school.

What led up to it? I had a similar feeling to the one I had before I went to the yoga school, the feeling of needing more guidance to move to another level, but not knowing how or where to access it. I was looking for help everywhere, feeling for it in the vibrations of people and events, searching for the key that would open the door. Then I found the book *Co-Creative Science* and used it as my key to open the door. Now I have school every day, even in my dreams. And it's lovely, so breathtakingly lovely, that it's a joy, and the graceful demands Nature puts on me are not a burden, but an honor.

FROM THE PWN HANDBOOK

Nature has skills that are outside of our expertise. Every project involves manifesting ideas into form, and Nature is the world's greatest authority on form manifestation. When working with Nature, you have access to a realm of knowledge outside your normal awareness. Projects flow more easily simply because you don't have to make all the decisions yourself. When questions arise, and you don't know the answer, or you're not sure of the best choice, you have this other resource that can give you answers. If you're willing to act on the answers, even without always completely understanding the reasons, it's very freeing. You don't have the burden of sole decision making.

We as humans are always making choices and decisions that arise out of our intentions. We work from intention. Nature's work operates differently. Nature unfolds manifestation from intention. On this planet, that often means that Nature unfolds manifestation from our intention. Nature unfolds manifestation with balance. When we take control, we can choose to use our free will to create an imbalance. For example, we can create a factory that spews pollution into the air. Nature will then attempt to correct the resulting imbalance. Nature would prefer to work with us to find another way of achieving the intended purpose of the factory.

When working with Nature, we aren't as likely to make decisions that are out of balance. If we're listening, Nature will stop us. We may not know why, but we'll be directed in another way. When I was first making flower essences, I questioned Nature about the exact procedure to be followed. Brandy is the traditional preservative, but I still asked, "Should I use brandy as a preservative?" and got the expected yes. Yet when questioning which kind of brandy to use, I found that none of the North American brandies was acceptable. Why? They were less expensive and would do just as good a job of preserving the essence.

I explained to my Nature team that if I bought French brandy, I would have to charge more for each bottle of essence. On this issue, Nature stood firm. I assumed they had their reasons, and chose the French brandy without understanding why.

Later I learned that the techniques for distilling brandy had been modified by American vintners in the 1930s. These methods were considered to be more appropriate for use with local grapes. However, they involve the use of higher heat, which is more destructive to the living essence of the brandy. I had a blind spot around this issue. Luckily, my partner had a larger perspective, which saved me from making an error in my processes.

RECEPTIVE HOMEOPATHY

Homeopathy opens a door, and the individual makes a choice to walk through the door or not. Not everyone wants the responsibility of being healed. When individuals choose health and walk through the door, it is their choice and their aspiration that bring change. Thus the often-reported sensation that homeopathy didn't act, that they "just got better."

Homeopathy is a receptive healing system. It does not impose, it does not choose. It merely clears the way for a possible choice. Homeopathy respects the free will of the individual. In this respect, homeopathy aligns with the laws of universal love that allow each soul freedom of choice.

REHEARSAL, THEN ACTION

Deep in the night, outside my normal awareness, it seems that I'm still working with my team. I sense that we're sometimes preparing for events to come. Even though my sleeping mind may be preparing to take certain steps, that doesn't guarantee that I'll carry them out as we planned. I still have free will, and we can't really know what my waking choice will be. It's important that I be given the opportunity for true choice without any conscious memory of our rehearsals.

I no longer believe that my walk into the desert and my

request to become a student of Nature was just something I decided to do one day. It wasn't just a response to reading *Co-Creative Science*. I see it now as a fundamental step to fulfilling my life purpose as called for in my soul contract, and as agreed to before my birth. And I believe that I had rehearsed it beforehand, probably many times, in my dreams. There were too many entities lined up and on board for it to be otherwise. My actions that day had the feel of sacred ceremony, of formal commitment, like a wedding or a baptism ceremony. I am profoundly grateful to all the beings who accompanied me that glorious day, helping me open the next chapter of my life.

In February an event occurs that, in retrospect, also has that rehearsed feeling. I get a preview of what the Mimzy Project may have in store for me.

LET THE ENERGY COME TO ME

An amazing, visionary day. Our small RV is deeply stuck in the snow on the mountain pass road leading to the Shamanic Valley campground. We have chains on all four wheels, but we don't realize that our four-wheel drive is broken until we're stuck. We work all day with shovels and a jack, but finally have to eat dinner and go to bed. No one has passed us on the road all day.

That night, my dreams are especially deep. I'm somewhere else—whether deep within the Earth or on another planet, I can't say. Suddenly I awake with a jerk. Skidmore has moved me over in the bed. The transition back into my body is so sudden that I feel almost in shock.

Around midnight flashing headlights wake me again. Three jeeps are passing us on the road. They slow down, and then pause for a moment. We run outside and Skidmore speaks to the man in the lead jeep, but he won't help. I run to the nearest jeep and knock on the window. The driver, Ross, asks me if I want him to pull the RV forward off the jack and to the center of the road. Yes! He takes a tow strap, hooks it to the front of our RV, and pulls us out. We start following him, but we are soon stuck again.

I am sitting in the passenger seat with an open connection to my Nature spirit and my White Brotherhood team. I sense that the energy is available to get us unstuck, if only it can be tapped and directed. It seems natural to "push" the energy, to try to force it to happen. I hear an inner voice telling me to "let the energy come to me." I repeat the phrase like a mantra, with an open heart chakra.

In my inner eye, I see spiraling coils of energy filling the space around me. I realize that my task is not to reach for the spiraling coils or try to pull them toward me, but rather to receptively generate a magnetism that will draw them toward me.

I'm still repeating the mantra, continuing to magnetically draw in the spiraling coils of energy and redirect them toward the situation of our stuck vehicle.

Ross backs up a bit to get a running start, but the RV is implacably stuck and the recoil jerks the jeep back. Ross comes to my window and I tell him that it seems that he has done all he can do. He asks for my flashlight and he and Skidmore begin shoveling snow out from under the RV. Then Ross tries pulling with the jeep again while I repeat my mantra, "Let the energy come to me," and continue to magnetize in the spiraling coils of energy. This time the jeep pulls the RV forward. We are able to follow Ross, sliding at times, until we are past the snow and mud.

We sleep the rest of the night at the campground turnoff, happy and grateful. I feel I learned something important that night, something I would need for the Mimzy Project and later in life.

DEEPENING AWARENESS: JOURNAL ENTRY,
FEBRUARY 20, 2010, SHAMANIC VALLEY CAMPGROUND

The unbelievable magic, mystery, and beauty of this place are sinking even more deeply into my soul. It seems that I am more aware of the ravens and other wildlife here than ever before. The colors of the landscape seem deeper. The part of me that connects to this desert seems more present. I'm grateful for the shift in me and the shift in the energy of the planet that is allowing this greater intensity of awareness to occur.

CHAPTER 2

THE MIMZY PROJECT

In March 2010, I'm part of a group preparing for the Mimzy Project. Since participants will be flying in from other parts of the United States and Canada, we are holding conference calls to make arrangements. Some people who cannot be present in person will be participating as *tethers*, supporting the project by sending us light and prayers.

Ursa has told me a bit about why she created the Mimzy Project. In April 2009, she was driving near Lake Shastina on an isolated back road. As she rounded a curve, the base of Mount Shasta came into view, and abruptly she heard voices. As if a radio station had suddenly come on with several stations bleeding through at once, voices poured into Ursa's head, asking her to bring herself and at least 12 others to Mount Shasta to join them on April 5, 2010.

None of us knows what will happen during the project. It could be something amazing, or it could be nothing.

MIMZY DREAM, MARCH 17, 2010

I wake up remembering the tail end of a dream. Today is the day that Sybil and Ursa are coming to lunch with me to discuss ley lines, or planetary meridians of electromagnetic energy, in preparation for the upcoming Mimzy Project.

Here is the end of the dream, as best as I can capture it on waking.

> *He was tall, rather regal looking and had indigenous-looking clothes and features. As if closing a long conversation or visit together, he said, "Don't worry, anyone can eat soup. Goodbye from the (garbled) Nation." The garbled word wasn't really garbled; it was just some language whose sounds I can't quite grasp. It had a guttural sound in it. Their name for their people. There was playfulness to his goodbye. I'm not worried about Ursa and Sybil liking the soup—I'm almost sure they will. But I do want our meeting to go well and for them to be pleased with it. He was joking. His tone was joking, but sweet, telling me not to worry. He clearly knows about our meeting and attaches some importance to it, even if only for my sake. I'm not sure, but I think he is a Mimzy being contacting me in a way I'll be comfortable with.*

Those preparing for the Mimzy Project are being contacted by beings that, from our descriptions of them, appear to be different from each other. Maybe we're contacting a vast confederation of beings. A confederation that can send each person a contact most suited to their individual needs. Of course, it may be that one being is appearing in different guises to different people. Perhaps. But my sense is that this is a confederation of beings working in unity with each other.

PRELUDE TO A CONVERSATION

Before I tell you about our luncheon conversation, it would be helpful to touch on some concepts that we didn't discuss. We didn't discuss them because we assumed that we were all aware of these concepts and we were tacitly acting in the light of them.

My motivation for joining the Mimzy Project was not predicated on any particular belief or assumption about how the universe works. I joined the Mimzy Project because when I heard Ursa and Sybil discuss it, my attention was hooked in a way impossible to ignore. I felt that I was being asked to join the project. Whether my higher self or my Nature team was asking me, I'm not sure. The feeling was that I was compelled to do it because of an inner sense of rightness that could not be denied.

That said, I want to state the cosmological assumptions that I was working with, even though I didn't know for certain if they were true.

The first assumption was that space is not empty as we sometimes think of it, and that a vacuum is not empty either. Waves of energy that the ancients called *aether* permeate all of space and all matter as well. Aether may be the hypothetical form of energy known as *dark energy* that science is currently seeking to understand. This aether is not spread evenly throughout space. Instead, there are bands of vibratory spectrums within the aether. We have a good sense of vibratory spectrums when dealing with sound and light. With sound, we recognize eight notes, with the first and eighth notes being the same, but an octave apart. With light we recognize eight colors, each one vibrating within a certain frequency rate. With aether, we call the analogous vibratory spectrums *densities*.

I was also working with the assumption that the solar system, as it is moving through space, is leaving one density, called the *third density,* and entering another, called the *fourth density.* This means that the vibration of aether throughout the solar system and in all matter within the solar system is increasing in frequency.

From our perspective, this change is sometimes referred to as the *ascension of the Earth,* even though it's actually happening to the entire solar system. The idea of ascension implies changes in consciousness as well as changes in frequency. Because consciousness is changing, old ways of doing things no longer work. People are demanding changes in politics, government, finance, agriculture, transportation, and communication.

Another way this has been said is that we are transitioning from the Piscean age to the Aquarian age. The Piscean age was a time of authoritarianism. Almost all structures in society were arranged hierarchically. Those in charge made decisions and took the lead, and those below them in the hierarchy followed instructions. There was great reverence for authority.

The Aquarian age is a time of collaboration. Almost all structures in society are changing to allow for shared decision making among groups of equals. The Aquarian age that we are entering is not better than the Piscean age. Both are equally right for their particular time. As a person's consciousness shifts to align with Aquarian principles, he or she will find that authoritarian hierarchies feel constricting and that collaborative decision making in groups feels more freeing.

A CONVERSATION ABOUT LEY LINES

Ursa and Sybil arrive at my house. They love the soup and the salad made from freshly picked greens from my garden.

After our lunch, I tell Ursa and Sybil what I consciously know about the ley lines. They are electromagnetic lines encircling the Earth both horizontally and vertically. Powerful vortices of energy are frequently located at the intersection of the ley lines. Mount Shasta, where the Mimzy Project is to take place, is one of the most powerful vortices on the planet, and is located at the intersection of several ley lines. I tell them that I believe the ley lines provide information to seekers.

The White Brotherhood has seeded information that we will need to meet new challenges into the ley lines. When a person on Earth is open to finding a new solution to a problem, information from the ley lines can be conveyed outside his or her conscious awareness. The person may suddenly see the problem in a new light or serendipitously find a piece of information that leads to a new solution. The ley lines provide information that allows users to expand their conscious perception of reality beyond their normal framework. One of the purposes of the Mimzy Project is for the participants to assist as conduits to embed more information into the ley line system. By information, I don't mean just data, but also consciousness. That is one reason we are planning to activate vortices of energy in a ring around the mountain. If the participants can hold a consciousness of love and unity during ceremonies at each vortex, then that consciousness can be more strongly seeded within the ley line system.

JOURNEY TO THE MOUNTAIN, MARCH 27, 2010

Today is the first of five days of preparation for the Mimzy

Project. Skidmore drives me to Claire's house, and I meet her for the first time. Sybil arrives. We pack our things and ourselves into her car, and begin our journey to the mountain. First we drive to a nearby town to meet Tavala and caravan with her. After a lunch stop, Claire takes the wheel. We've seen Tavala occasionally when we've passed her, and we know that she's blissed out, singing chants and songs to God. As we approach the first exit to the City of Mt. Shasta, both cars are in the right lane. Tavala's white car is ahead of us, and there are a couple of cars between us and her.

Sybil tells Claire that we need to pass Tavala immediately or she'll miss the exit. At the same time, the traffic on the freeway is slowing. There is a police car ahead, zigzagging across the lanes, slowing the cars down. It feels as though time is slowing too, and everything becomes quiet. All the cars appear to be moving in slow motion. Then we look for Tavala, and we can't see her. She's not there. We scan the freeway and surrounding cars and finally find her a couple of cars behind us.

Later Tavala tells us that she had the same experience. We were behind her, and then she couldn't see us, and then she found that we were ahead of her. Claire asks her if she ever moved into the left lane. Could she have passed us that way? Tavala is sure that she was never in the left lane.

It occurs to me that Tavala could have teleported to another dimension and when she came back, we had moved forward and were now ahead of her. I ask my guides and receive a different answer. They say that Sybil, Claire, and I teleported to another dimension and when we came back, we were ahead of Tavala. If this is true, none of us can consciously remember our journey to the other dimension or what transpired there.

Although this occurrence sounds mysterious, I believe it

only seems that way. We are embedded at all times in a reality that is beyond space, time and description. We can encompass in our mind only that part of reality that we can process and integrate at the time. If something occurs that is beyond our normal expectation, but we can still identify and integrate it to some extent, we will perceive it as an extraordinary but understandable event. Our understanding may be distorted, but we will still know that something happened. If something is beyond the bounds of what we understand to be possible, we will not be able to perceive it at all. We will not be conscious of it; it will be as if it never happened.

I choose to believe that the interdimensional beings that we were working with in the Mimzy Project took an action that moved us outside our normal time and space for a moment, and that action was done for a purpose and with our soul level consent.

Later in a shop, I find a stone to help with a headache that I've developed during the day. I figure it's a reaction to the higher vibration that I'm now experiencing. My guides help me select a blue crystocolla stone.

We arrive at Stewart Mineral Springs, where five of us are to spend three nights before moving to Mount Shasta Ranch when the whole group arrives. We meet Kalia, who has driven from the Mount Hood area. I tell Kalia that I'm not clear on how we are to find the energy points. Kalia says that is her job, so I give her the maps that Ursa emailed me. Sybil also gives her maps showing where she and Ursa had checked out possible sites the previous summer. Most of those areas are now inaccessible due to snow. I'm very tired, but I'm so caught up in talking to Kalia about the maps that I can hardly tear myself away to go to bed.

We Are the Scouts, March 28, 2010

The Mountain. We are here. Claire, Tavala, Kalia, Sybil, and me. We are the scouts sent to lead the way. Heights of joy, depths of sorrow, serenity, and upset, dissension, and unity—all are here dancing with us.

Structure. I love it and I'd love to bring it forward and anchor it among us. Not as a limiting unbending thing as some fear, but as a beautiful cathedral holding the space for us.

Expectations. There are 26 people in the Mimzy Project, who are coming with expectations—or at least with one expectation: that something profound will happen. And it will. We will experience the power of the mountain and the truth of unity between ourselves and unity with all that is.

My headache is gone. It resolved during a session with my White Brotherhood Medical Assistance Program (MAP) team. During the session, I was guided to place the crystocolla stone over my throat chakra. I'm grateful for the help and the relief.

We drive in Kalia's car down the road to an area where there is cell phone reception to make calls. Kalia points out the lenticular clouds over Mount Shasta and explains how to tell if they are spaceships giving off cold rather than ordinary clouds. She says she saw several spaceships the previous day, escorting her on her journey. Today large ships are coming into, or leaving, the mountain.

We drive into town to meet with a local group called the Wise Women. We don't know anyone in their group, and we're a little reluctant to go, because we're tired and we want to rest.

But we talk to Ursa on the phone and she says it's important that we meet them. So we find their meeting place and introduce ourselves to them. Zara is their leader and she guides us in chanting the 72 names of God that have been collected in the book *The Seventy-two Sacred Names of the Myriad Expressions of the Living God* by J.J. Hurtak.

We take turns choosing a page in the book by feeling for the "right" page without looking at it. Then we chant the name given on that page. As we chant, the sunlit room appears to shimmer with light and we all begin to feel lighter.

Zara asks, "Can you feel this? It's working."

Later I learn that the Wise Women had never met in that way before, and that they never do it again. Meeting Zara sets events into motion that subsequently resonate out into my future.

Later that evening, Claire, Tavala, and I are in the room that Tavala and I are sharing. Sybil and Kalia have gone to phone Ursa. We're concerned; there is tension within our group. As a newcomer to the group, I don't understand why this is happening. I'm clear that there is nothing helpful that I can do directly.

I'm relieved when Claire suggests that we send the violet flame of Saint Germain to Sybil, Kalia, and Ursa. I ask Tavala to lead us in the meditation because I don't know much about the violet flame. Tavala guides us in visualizing a violent flame around the three of us and around Sybil, Kalia and Ursa. Then we meditate for maybe half an hour. Afterward we feel much better; the energy has shifted for us.

I remember that we have downloaded information that one of the Mimzy participants received about unity. She had emailed it to us, and I printed it. I read it aloud for Claire and Tavala, which also seems to lift the energy.

Here is part of the download.

You are coming not just to serve, but to be uplifted, restored, and loved into remembrance. Let unity be embodied among you and anchored in the Earth. Together, you will remember yourselves and each other.

You have misunderstood what it means to forgive. The old paradigm is based on the illusion that there is something wrong with you. Believing this, to forgive would seem to reinforce it. So you hold on to the perceived wrongdoing, hoping that it was not your fault, rather the fault of the other. The whole notion of fault and blame is in itself another misconception. There is only light and darkness. Darkness and forgetfulness are the illusion of right and wrong, separation of self and other, separation from God. All war is about self-hatred; the war within. We invite you to put down your arms, drop the armor and embrace yourself with love. Notice your daily conflicts, what you complain about, and find fault with in yourself and in others. Then drop your arms. Literally drop your arms by your sides. Feel the armor drop and dissolve; allow the shield to embrace you.

You are in fact so magnificent, so radiant, so pure, so loving that you could be blinded by your own light. Who you are is pure love, nothing more, nothing less.

We invite you to open, see, sense, and hear that which you truly are. We are here to reflect that to you.

AT THE HEADWATERS, MARCH 29, 2010

Kalia, the Goddess, fierce of mien, is unstoppable. Tavala is like a tender unicorn. Standing at the headwaters of the

Sacramento River, Kalia calls the spirits, the masters, the directions, and they come, creating a towering vortex of energy. Kalia spreads her arms, curving them to hold the crescendo of energy. I hold my arms wide, embracing the energy. Energy spirals upwards from my crown chakra and from the crown of the cedar tree at whose base I sit. Music somewhat like violins emits from the eye of the tempest.

Kalia, controlling the energy, looks like Moses parting the waters. At the moment of maximum energy, Kalia blows on the energy. In an instant, the energy emanating from the vortex changes from intense to diffuse balmy calm. All is bathed in love and violet light. We ride in waves of warm, loving energy, soaking all the glorious softness into ourselves.

Later we are told that the fifth-density water in the headwaters has been intensified 1,000 times by the energy field Kalia called in, and we are instructed to drink this elixir. We drink the living water, saturating our cells.

One of the Wise Women relates a story about the headwaters from an event called the Harmonic Convergence, which occurred in August 1987. The first globally synchronized meditation, it was held at sacred sites worldwide, including at Mount Shasta.

There is a legend that descendants of people from the ancient continent of Lemuria, which sunk into the Pacific Ocean, live today in an underground city called Telos, located beneath Mount Shasta. The people of Telos are believed to be spiritually and technologically advanced. It is their spaceships that can sometimes be seen entering and leaving the mountain. During the weekend of the Harmonic Convergence, a Lemurian temple was built in a higher dimension of the headwaters and has been waiting to be anchored when the right people came.

Kalia believes this temple may have been anchored into place today, because she heard and experienced a sound, as if something physical was clicking into place. I feel honored to take my place alongside the many people and beings who have worked together in unity over many years to build and activate this temple.

A Visit to an Underground City, March 30, 2010

The next day, I attempt to visit the underground city of Telos. Early in the morning, we gather at the gazebo of Stewart Mineral Springs, where the red source water and white source water mix. Kalia invokes the spirits. I want to visit the underground city, so I send a telepathic message to the people of Telos asking them if I may make an energetic journey there. I receive the answer: "We are in the trees and the water. We can make contact with you anywhere." For a moment, I'm seized with doubt. I may not have the spiritual qualities needed to go there, but I tell myself to drop this thought.

I continue to focus on the meditation, and feel myself drawn upwards energetically. I'm afraid to exhale, as if I might fall down a rabbit hole. As I release my breath, energetically I descend part way into the mountain, then, as I breathe in and release again, I descend much further. I am there, in the city of Telos. I see nothing with my eyes, but feel the people of Telos all around me. I greet each one as if we're at a party, "I'm so happy to see you. I'm so happy to see you. I'm so happy to see you ..." I feel their love and support, and most amazingly, I feel a passionate overflowing love for them. I yell into the cosmos, "I love you!"

After a time of drinking in their love and support, I feel myself snapped back into an awareness of my body, like the snapping of a rubber band. I take a moment to look around me. I am still standing in the gazebo with the other Mimzy scouts. I close my eyes again and return to meditation.

Music like a harpsichord is playing. Other people are here in spirit, energetically stuck to me like Velcro: first just the Mimzy Project team, but then others. All those who have the desire and can hold the energy are here, connecting with the loving and compassionate beings of Telos. The unity, joy, and love are indescribable. I am so grateful to God and to the beings of Telos for those precious moments of joy and deep connection. The connection that we felt that day is eternal—it will not pass away.

WE INITIATE THE VORTICES, MARCH 30-31, 2010

Sybil and Claire are selecting crystals and making other arrangements for the larger group that will be arriving the next day. Kalia, Tavala, and I are activating vortices of energy in a ring around Mount Shasta. Later we will perform a ceremony at each vortex with the entire Mimzy group.

We begin at the cross-country ski area on the mountain, each of us connecting our energy strongly to the center of the mountain. At first, the power of the connection makes me a little nauseous, like sea sickness, but that soon passes. Then we drive down the mountain to create each of the vortices as follows.

At the southeastern point off Highway 89: We name this vortex Jolly Point because it is a light-spirited place. Kalia invokes the energy and I find part of myself back in Telos. I'm both inside the mountain and at Jolly Point. I begin playing with the energy, my two bodies playing patty cake with each other and then passing energy back and forth on a rope of light. Later I connect with the Nature spirits and tell them that I represent those who would work in partnership with Nature. They show me what our Earth would be like if all humankind were doing that. They show me a beautiful pyramid mountain towering above fertile fields dotted with neat, comfy-looking farmhouses, healthy crops, and enough water and energy for everyone.

At Lake Siskiyou, the southwestern point: We are grounding a vortex of energy. This time I'm within the earth. My body is like a crystal in the earth. Part of me is also within the mountain and another part at Jolly Point. The three of us take turns spinning the rope of light back and forth to each other. Later I learn that Kalia has called in spirits of dolphins and whales, and that Tavala sees them frolicking in the lake together.

The next day, we continue initiating the vortices.

At Lower Klamath Lake: We are on the viewing platform of a wildlife refuge. Flocks of birds are continually arriving and leaving from the marshy waters below. As soon as Kalia brings in the energy, I'm flying, my wings exiting from my heart chakra in back, flapping to the pulse of my heart energy. I fly to the mountain, then in turn to the other points where we have opened vortices of energy: Jolly Point, the headwaters of the Sacramento River, Lake Siskiyou, Lake Shastina, and the yet unknown point to the north of the mountain that we will soon find. I fly to all these places, crisscrossing between them.

A couple then joins us on the viewing platform. The man talks to Kalia, telling her about his love for birds, especially for the ones he calls "the yellow-headed birds." He tells us that insects are eating the wood of a lean-to he built, which just goes to show he shouldn't have built it in the first place because, "Mother Nature must have her way." As he leaves, he calls this place Bird Heaven.

After the man and his wife depart, Kalia restarts the energy, and I experience a connection with the man. I sense that he understands the importance of working with Nature. I connect to all the people on the planet who are awake and open and want to find a better way for humanity to live. The Mimzy Project is for them: to make higher-density dynamics more accessible to those who are searching.

Later, we open the energy at the final point. It's clear that the Mimzy beings would have preferred a nearby lookout, but there's too much snow for us to get there. This place off Highway 97 in a circle of cedar trees is a likeable substitute. As Kalia opens the energy, the beings are here doing acrobatic stunts, like cartwheels and somersaults. After a time, I am energetically skiing on the mountain and doing something like somersaults on my skis. I jump up, flip around in a circle, and land on my skis. We are celebrating the successful location and opening of vortices at each of the points.

Kalia, Tavala, and I have done all but two of the points. Ursa has done Lake Shastina. The Mimzy tethers, a group of people supporting us remotely from around the globe, will do Medicine Lake energetically, since there's too much snow to access it physically at this time.

We call this final vortex Rumbling Point because Kalia could feel the earth shaking at this place. I think my mind must have interpreted the shaking as tumbling acrobatics. It's amazing to me that I experienced the earth shaking as frolicking on skis. I hope I'll remember that, and not be afraid if the earth moves again.

Back at Mount Shasta Ranch, most of our group of

22 women and four men has arrived. We have the first of the fabulous meals that a crew of Mimzy participants has prepared for us. Each person is scheduled to work on two or three meals during the course of the project. The meal crews are directed by Jerri, who we call Captain Cook. Throughout the project, Jerri remains at the Mount Shasta Ranch to plan meals while the rest of us leave for our daily adventures.

After dinner we gather. Tess sings "Give Yourself to Love" by Kate Wolf on her guitar. I feel that Kate's precept to "give yourself to love if love is what you're after" is a good touchstone for how I want to live the following precious days with this luminous group of people.

HEADWATERS CEREMONY, APRIL 1, 2010

It is one of the best days of my life. We arrive at the headwaters with our Mimzy group and some of the Wise Women.

I think of my older son, Dickon, strongly, out of the blue, as if he is trying to connect with me. I wonder if it's my imagination, so as a comparison, I think of my younger son and my husband. It's quite different. I'm thinking *about* my son Thor and *about* Skidmore, but Dickon is *here*, present in a direct way. Energetically I ask him if he wants to attend the ceremony, and he says yes.

A Native American man appears among us suddenly. We didn't see him approach, but there are other people nearby filling water bottles at the spring, so we may not have noticed his arrival. To us, it seems magical. He asks Kalia if he may join us and she says, "Of course." He begins chanting and playing a drum as Kalia opens the energy. Then there is chanting all around us. Ancient male voices are chanting, their voices coming from we know not where.

I ask to see a Mimzy being with my inner eye. I can hear them and feel them, but I want to see them. After a time I see Naja, the cobra. He is a Mimzy being and he is here. I am happy and overflowing with gratitude that Dickon is also with me for the beautiful ceremony.

Afterward I ask Dickon if he wants to disconnect, but he says no. So I ask him if he wants to go to the ski area with us, and he says yes.

After lunch we drive the beautiful road to the ski area. After walking in the snow a bit, Kalia opens the energy with the intent for us to connect with the mountain. I find myself drawn down into the earth. I open my heart to the mountain and all the beings there. Dickon is still entrained with me. Claire starts chanting, "Om," and others begin singing and chanting Hindu prayers. Everything is for the glory of God and the oneness of all creation. My heart is overflowing with love and gratitude, and my absolute joy that Dickon is here with us. As I walk back to the parking lot, I ask him if he is ready to disconnect, and he says yes. I estimate that he was with us from about 10 a.m. until about 3 p.m.

After a delicious dinner, we join with some of the Wise Women and other local people for a drumming session. We drum ecstatically for about an hour using many drums and a gong. In my inner vision, I see Naja again and also an extraterrestrial. Later Kalia tells me that Mimzy beings, ETs, and a spaceship were with us.

GOOD FRIDAY, APRIL 2, 2010

Good Friday is a day of reflection. It snows most of the day while we stay warm and cozy at Mount Shasta Ranch. I write the following in my journal:

*We know not who we are, we who create war, we
who create financial turmoil through greed, we who
foment dissension and division for our own ends. We
know not who we are. We do not see ourselves as we
really are, as beings of light. Today I drop all resentments,
all accusations—even the accusations I make toward
myself. They are gone. If a person has wronged another,
they know not who they are. Neither the one wronged
nor the one who wrongs can be harmed. Let us go forth
in the beauty that we are and hold each other harmless.
As did the Christ, so do I offer myself as a servant of love.*

*The Mimzy Project is to anchor remembrance of
who we are: pure love, on Earth. And so it is.*

That evening Zara and the Wise Women come to the
Ranch and we chant some of the 72 names of God. I am
elated to share this powerful and ecstatic experience with the
whole group.

WE SET THE CRYSTALS, APRIL 3, 2010

The next day, Holy Saturday, we travel with the entire
Mimzy group to each of the vortices to ceremonially set crystals at each site.

Bird Heaven: We go onto the viewing platform in groups.
The crystals are already imbibed with our essence because
we previously meditated with them, holding each crystal to
one of our chakras. I take the lapis lazuli stone, reawaken my
essence in it, and fling it into the lake. Kalia sees a giant crystal
pyramid descend and anchor over this site.

Rumbling Point: I bury amethyst here. Kalia sees a pillar
of light descending on our clearing.

Lake Shastina: We have lunch here. I see a Mimzy being that looks like a tiger near the outhouse. Later we form a V-shape by lining ourselves up into two diagonal lines. I toss the aquamarine crystal in the lake. Kalia says we all energetically rode over the lake in a triangle-shaped vehicle.

Jolly Point: We experience the same lightness of spirit we felt here before. Two bushes still guard the hollowed-out stump. We offer our love to the mountain, leaving our crystals in openings in the tree stump. I leave the Lemurian crystal here. As I wait for others to place their crystals, I see a door in my inner sight, which slightly opens, as if inviting me in. I walk up to the door, push it open, and walk in. That's the end of the vision, but I feel that I have accepted an invitation to some future event or journey. After the ceremony, some in the group have a snowball fight, letting off steam and reflecting the playful energy of the place.

Lake Siskiyou: The loveliness of this site hasn't changed. I feel deep love for the mountain and the lake. I leave the Herkimer crystal in the lake. Ursa sings a song the Mimzy beings taught her.

> *Holy, holy, holy*
> *Sacred Mother guide me*
> *In your great mystery*
> *Hold my gentle soul*

It's clear to us that the Mimzy beings are celebrating the completion of the setting of the crystals. After the ceremony is over, I take a quick energetic trip back into the mountain, just popping in for a minute to give those in Telos my love.

Back at the ranch, my heart is singing thank you, thank

you, thank you. In my inner sight, I dive deep into Lake Siskiyou and gracefully resurface. It feels like a baptism. Holy, holy, holy.

I see the door again. An adventure to be continued.

EASTER SUNDAY, APRIL 4, 2010

Getting ready to go to the Mount Shasta Pyramid, my Nature guides keep calling me back to my room because I don't have all that is needed. I understand that I am to take the Perelandra Soil Balancing Kit.

The Mimzy Project group drives to the pyramid in the snow. It's Easter Sunday, a day of remembrance and reconciliation. The part of me that thinks about danger, safety, and prudence is concerned because several cars don't have chains or four-wheel drive. Normally I would advise people not to drive in these conditions, but our clarity of purpose is too strong to be denied.

We are a group of 25 people in love. In love with God, in love with multidimensional beings and guides, in love with our assignment, and in love with each other.

When we drive into the parking area, I am the first person out of the car, and I greet the man waiting for us, the builder of this pyramid. Meeting his eyes, I experience an electrical contact between us. This person is so powerful that his eyes are like lasers. As Ursa arrives I tell him that she is one of our leaders, and he moves to greet her.

It is cold and dark inside the pyramid. Sybil has loaned me a warm shawl, for which I am deeply grateful. People are shifting around, trying to find the appropriate spot for their unique energy within this pyramid.

I am clear that I have been assigned to do the soil balancing process before we begin, and again before we leave. I unzip the plastic bag containing the Perelandra Soil Balancing Kit. The sound of the crinkly plastic disturbs the person next to me, and she tells me to stop. Stopping is not an option, so I continue with the test, finding that two soil balancers, cottonseed meal and dolomite lime, are needed. I hold each in my hand in turn, offering them to Pan to infuse their energies as needed to balance the soil beneath the pyramid. It is likely that our ceremony will use some of the soil nutrients, so I will rebalance them before I leave.

I can't remember all the angelic dreams we enacted that day. We sang songs of love and yearning. We sang songs of adoration and transcendence. Our songs were drawn from many traditions: Anglo American, Celtic, Native American, and South American. We sang ancient songs and ones newly birthed in the moment, songs accompanied by dances of the snake and the eagle. We move in groups into the eye of the pyramid, bringing with us our most cherished dreams. Dreams of peace for our planet. Dreams enfolding and supporting our world leaders. Dreams of an abundance of clean food and water for our children and grandchildren. Dreams of unity between ourselves and the beings of other dimensions and other planets.

Then, at the right time, in a moment after a crescendo of energy, it is done. We are complete. We have no timepiece with us, but later we learn that the completion was precisely at the end of the prescribed two hours that we were to be in the pyramid.

I quickly test the soil again and find that we have used three soil elements, which I offer to Pan for replacement. Later, I notice that one of the elements used was phosphorus, which

I have read can be needed when an extraterrestrial spaceship is present. Although I did not see a ship in my inner eye, some of my companions tell me that one was present.

As we are about to descend out of the pyramid, Martha asks the men to go first and "safe-port" the women down the ladder. Some of us are wondering if this is really necessary, but Ursa reminds us that Martha is our elder and to listen to her words. So we have the delightful and wonderfully balanced sensation of being escorted down from this majestic pyramid under the protection of our loving and gentle men.

Return to the Sacred Headwaters, April 5, 2010

The next day is a settling in day. Each of us shares a personal part of our journey. Kalia thinks a monograph about this project could be written. She asks each person to email her some part of their story, including their experiences leading up to the start of the project.

At lunch some of us discuss how the color of our crystal pendants has changed. Mine was clear when I received it on March 31. We had each dipped our pendant into the headwaters on April 1. A decorative metal piece holds the top of the crystal and allows it to be strung on a necklace. The opposite end of the crystal terminates in a point. Now my crystal has a more violet hue, especially at the point, and has acquired a violet striation three-quarters of the way toward the point. Tess and others have noticed the same thing about their pendants.

We return to the headwaters for the closing of the Mimzy Project. We each put a few crystals on our tree stump altar. During the ceremony I see spinning mandalas and human and animal spirits in my inner vision. I fill myself with love and light, sending light out my crown. When we each retrieve our crystals, I take mine to the tree that helped me when we opened the portal at this place. I put my arms around it, removing my glasses so I can get my cheek closer to it. I'm filled with love and gratitude for this magnificent tree! After a time, I take a few steps to the bank, send my essence into the crystals, and throw them into the water. I come back to the tree, say goodbye, and tear myself away. This is the first of many difficult goodbyes.

Later in a local shop, a crystal calls to me. I'm still connected to the Nature spirits and White Brotherhood members from the ceremony. They want that crystal. It isn't one on display; it's on a low shelf behind the counter. At first I think they want one of the smaller crystals on the shelf above. I'm a little taken aback when I realize the size and power of the one they want. Also by the realization that this is their idea of what would be useful. They must have big plans!

I ask the price and find that I can afford the crystal. I buy it and put it in my backpack. The entities are like little kids with a new toy. I, on the other hand, am soon feeling the effects of having it on my person. I ask them to help me select a stone to buy that will soothe the transition for me. They select green calcite, which starts helping immediately. They also tell me to buy a rutilated quartz sphere for my office. This stone is known for its help in diagnosing illness. Just as I'm paying for it, Kalia shows me another rutilated quartz crystal and says she was told to show it to me. I have some regret that I haven't bought that one instead, and I think that I may return later to buy it as well.

Dinner is companionable and relaxed. In the background, we are all aware of the coming separations. Our field is bonded; we are all part of something greater forever. Each of us is connected more strongly to certain others of us, but the field is one and will hold.

Parting, April 6, 2010

In the early morning's dawning, I say goodbye to my new friend, Sky, not knowing when I'll see her again. I ask her to keep in touch and tell her "I want to know how your life unfolds and to hear about all the great things you will do in the future." I don't know then that our next adventure together is only six months away.

Our group meets for breakfast at a diner. We take up nearly half of one of the two main dining rooms, bringing an energy that's different from the rest of the place. It's almost as if there is an invisible pyramid of exuberance over our part of the room. Later, one member of our group tells me that she returned to this restaurant a few days later and was surprised to find an ordinary diner.

After breakfast, I buy lovely postcards of the mountain, and then wait in the parking lot, enjoying a magnificent view of the Mother Mount Shasta herself. Today there are no clouds around her and her snow-capped peak glistens in the sunny morning.

After a time, I return to the diner to find that several people are trying to process what happened at yesterday's gathering when we were sharing our personal reflections. Each of us had spoken for a few minutes, saying what was in our heart at the close of our project. During her share, Celeste said that we should each speak with care because sometimes people can be hurt by our words, even when that's not our intention. Ursa interrupted her, saying that hurt is not part of her experience and people need to refuse to accept it. She said that spiritual teachers can rip people up one side and down another and that the recipient of this is being given an opportunity to grow. Celeste said that she felt disrespected because her share was interrupted. The aftermath of this encounter is still rippling through the group, and people are trying to make sense of it and deal with their feelings around it. My own thought is that we need more time to process it and that each person will find his or her own way of integrating it.

We return to the shops and Kalia helps me find the right rutilated crystal to buy. We spend a lot of time in the store, and it's difficult for me because I know it will be painful to say goodbye to Kalia. She asks me to call her the next day, which eases the pain a bit, but it still hurts to hug her and tear myself away.

Sybil, Claire, and I begin our drive home. Sybil suggests we do a completion exercise during the drive. We take turns sharing our experiences of the project. What was pleasurable, what was not pleasurable, what we are thankful for, and what did we receive from it? And finally, what will be unfolded in each of our lives five years from now because of the Mimzy Project. My response to this last one is, "Compassionate healing with justice." I sense a deepening of my role as a healer in the future, and in that role, a balancing of compassion and justice.

We reach my house around 5 p.m. I'm happy knowing I will see Sybil and Claire again soon. I'm also happy to be home, happy knowing that my husband Skidmore and my dog Skip will soon be home, and that life will be back to "normal," but never the same.

CHAPTER 3

THE DOMAIN OF LOVE

In mid-April of 2010, the Eyjafjallajökull volcano in Iceland erupted, spewing ash over a large area of Northern Europe. European air flights were grounded for several days, affecting more than 100,000 travelers. I awoke early in the morning of April 22, vividly remembering a dream in which I seemed to be floating high above a small island in a dark sea. A lighthouse below me was the prominent feature of the island. Later that day, I channeled these words about my dream.

A BOLSTERING: JOURNAL ENTRY, APRIL 22, 2010

Ve Skerries, off the coast of Shetland. You were there in your dream. There is a grid there and we wanted you to be there as a bolstering. We knew you could do this because of other times when we were able to employ you as a lightning rod for placing energy into the grid, at the Ravens' Canyon, at Codfish Falls, and at Mount Shasta. Your past life as a Viking was helpful, but not necessary. We can work with you anywhere on the Earth.

You are a being, a citizen, of the Earth. We work through earth beings that align in loving cooperation with us. This is rightful. We do not interfere in the affairs of humankind.

Humans have free will. Only when enough earth beings want and accept our healing can we work through you. So even though you are the instrument, know that you are also a representative of all those on your planet who want this earth healing to happen. That is why you had the two experiences, one at Bird Heaven and the other in the pyramid. You also experienced this in the gazebo where the red source water and the white source water flow together. In each of those moments you felt as though millions of people of good heart, who are yearning for healing for the planet, were gathered closely around you. You felt that they were attached tightly to you as if with Velcro. This was a true experience: You are connected with them and you have their support for what you are doing. Just as people vote for their representative in your government, they have voted for you to represent them. This gives us the consent we need to act through you.

So Ve Skerries is a bolstering, and yes, it is related to the volcano and the shifting in that area. Ursa will be pleased to know that the bolstering is helping protect her beloved Ireland as well as Scotland and Norway. These shifts must happen, the energy must be released. We are working with you to mitigate damage that isn't essential to the upliftment of your planet. One result of your group's work in the pyramid was a stabilizing of the Cascade Range and a deflection of energy to an area of lesser harm. The energy was reflected to a less inhabited area.

Next week, you will be given an opportunity to do some more clearing in the Sutter Buttes. Your companion Naja, the cobra, will help you there just as the magnificent conifer tree helped you at the headwaters of the Sacramento River.

Last night in your sleep, you met again with your companions at the headwaters. This meeting was for renewal and remembrance. It is a touchstone that you can return to that energizes yourself and your connection to the others of the Mimzy group.

The lookout tower at Crater Lake—we will look from that point together. We will see from there with your eyes and you will see from there with our eyes. You will see what we see. Such beauty. Your companions from the nature kingdom will accompany you. You will see love and balance in action. Crater Lake and Jolly Point are two points of a triangle. We will help you locate the third point. There are points in Lassen Volcanic National Park and the Grand Tetons that will unfold themselves later. We can't reveal everything today, because things need to evolve in their own sequence and timing. You will recognize it at the right time and it will be a learning, and growing, opportunity for you.

Kalia has questioned if the lava tubes at Mount Shasta are connected with lava tubes in the Sutter Buttes. These chambers are connected with intent. You won't discover the connection by looking in the third-dimensional world. They are connected energetically because the mountains themselves have chosen the connection. When you are in the Sutter Buttes, your energy will be informed by the energy from Mount Shasta that is within you. The mountains will recognize this energy within you and will receive you as a friend. Walk there with awareness and an assignment will be presented to you. Later when you see the mountains from your window, you will remember the day you spent there and will experience a feeling of gladness, connectedness and love.

Love, love, radiant love
Shine, shine through me.
Guide me always through the dream of life.
Return me home.

THE SUTTER BUTTES

We have come to this place in response to Wendy's invitation, Kalia's prompting, and the instructions received while writing in my journal last week. Sybil has wisely brought a crystal. Without thinking about it, I have brought water from the headwaters in my water bottle. The beloved entities make it easy for us to find the vortex we are seeking. A long, thin cloud points to the spot like a slanting finger in the sky. We ask our human guides to leave the path and lead the group up the hill. We angle northward toward and slightly northeast of the sacred North Butte, home of ancient spirits.

Reaching a lunch spot, Sybil and I leave the others, moving uphill and to our right. I'm climbing strongly, breathing hard. I'm excited and magnetized toward the place. It's drawing me to it with its magnificent energy and power. As I climb nearer, the energy suddenly opens much more strongly in me. I feel Kalia's presence. I'm weeping with joy and with the knowledge that all is unfolding as intended.

Now Sybil has reached the place where I felt the energy intensifying. She says, "Kalia is here." I'm happy for this validation that Sybil and I are sharing the same experience.

I reach the energy center and tell Sybil, "This is it."

The grass is swirling, a powerful energy surrounds us. We are in the eye of the vortex; the swirling grass is the outward sign of its spiraling energy.

I immediately send my energy strongly into the vortex

and down into the grid. I connect energy through the grid to the glorious Mother mountain, Mount Shasta herself. Sybil hands me the crystal. I send my essence into it and return it to her. She finds the place it belongs and buries it there.

In a voice of exaltation, I declare, "We claim this mountain for the domain of love." A bold audacious statement, rightly uttered.

Sybil says a yogic prayer. Then I pray the words from last week's writing. I think I mix the words up a bit, but it doesn't matter. The mountain and the beings know.

"Love, love, radiant love
Shine, shine through me.
Guide me through the dream of life.
Return me home."

Sybil prays, "Shanti, shanti, shanti." It is done. I am overflowing with radiant energy and happiness.

Then I see Cicely, a member of our larger group. She is taking our picture. I had no idea that someone else is nearby. I beckon to her saying "Cicely, come here." She walks up to us and I ask her to stand in the exact place I had been standing. I move aside a foot or two, and I'm surprised to find the energy is lessened somewhat even that small distance away. The energy is still swirling, as are the grasses.

Cicely is palpably drinking in the energy. She's like a thirsty person on a hot day drinking a cool glass of lemonade. "Oh," she says, "I needed that." She has a walking staff from Kauai, decorated with Hawaiian words and signs. This she twists into the ground, connecting the energy of the Love Islands with this vortex.

I take my headwaters water and pour it on our hands and the ground. We are guided to find and take nearby rocks. I take one for myself and one for Kalia. Sybil takes one for herself and one for Ursa.

Later, our guide tells me that my rocks are rhyolite, a relatively light volcanic rock that rises to the surface of the earth. As she is telling me this, my husband finds an obsidian rock in the middle of a wide dirt road. She tells him that it's rare to find obsidian on the Sutter Buttes, and that the rock is for him to take. He questions if someone maybe brought it there and accidentally dropped it on the road. Otherwise, wouldn't someone else have found and taken it before now? I reassure him that the beings want him to have it, that's why he found it.

Later in the car, I tell him that I find myself in the same predicament as him: I need to acknowledge and validate my own power and authority. This is what my life is now, so I need to replace my old picture of myself with an expanded one. After all, there's no going back, so I just need to get over it. I'm hoping Skidmore will consider the possibility that the obsidian rock is a gift in recognition of his work with Nature.

The hike back to the car is glorious. The trees are shining with an ineffable light. The mother cows are heavy with milk, with suckling babies by their side. The joy and beauty of nature is arrayed in delightful symmetry all around us. We leave for the "real world" with grateful hearts.

LUPINS: JOURNAL ENTRY, MAY 5, 2010

Lupins. Vibrant blue clusters of lupins. On their roots they carry a colony of microbes that fertilizes them, and in return the lupins feed the microbes their sugar. Lupins are the first colonizers of the dead blasted-out ground left after a volcano, the first life to return to the barren volcanic wasteland.

They are a toehold that restarts the cycle of life. Today, thirty years after the cataclysm of Mount Saint Helens, life in all its amazing diversity abounds on that mountain. I am grateful to life, that she never stops, never gives up, and always returns, bringing us hope and joy.

The time of awaiting impending events is necessary. Many factors must align for us to get the biggest growth surge for the amount of energy expended. We want to work as efficiently as we can to expose the earth and its living residents to as little damage as possible, while fully completing the required changes.

The level of cooperation in this enterprise is not as high as we would desire, there is a lot of opposition and digging in of heels. This will eventually pass. Many are now letting go of compromises they've made with the way things have been, compromises that were a necessary adjustment to life on Earth as it was, but that are no longer necessary and no longer serve. Others are so heavily compromised that they don't recognize their perceived reality as a compromise. They are currently enmeshed in struggle.

For those who can joyfully jettison their compromises, life is becoming even more magnificent. The beauty of the Earth is more palpable and luminous than ever before. The song of birds is sweeter. The chirping of crickets in the field is more joyous. The whole of nature is harmonizing with the higher vibration the Earth is experiencing. Lovely vibrations of sound and light are emanating from the planet out into the cosmos. The view of Earth from space is becoming ever more enchanting.

Those who relinquish their outdated compromises become calmer and filled with gratitude. They are centered in the eye of the storm as upheaval unfolds. Now is a time of infinite possibilities.

You are creating the world you want. You are dreaming it into reality. Choose your thoughts and activities wisely. Surround yourself with love and beauty. Live in alignment with the natural world. The choices you make now are creating your new lifestyle, government, religion, community, occupations, and economy. Beyond these changes lies a responsibility unrecognized by most on the planet. The unity of humankind must solidify before the citizens of the Earth can properly represent themselves as citizens of the universe. The details of what needs to happen are beyond your grasp, but know that there is a rightful place for humankind in the interplanetary councils. It may be helpful to consider this honor and responsibility that awaits you as you work toward peace and the unity of humankind.

Volcanoes and other Earth changes will come. Destruction will happen. Lupins and other early colonizers will return the barren earth to life. A more joyous time approaches.

FROM THE PWN HANDBOOK

There's a certain feeling that's hard to define that you get when you're pushing for an answer. You may feel like you're working with Nature. You may be telling yourself that you just want the answer so you can do things Nature's way. In reality, you're trying to use your personal power to get what you want: an answer now. That way you can make your plans, and maybe meet some kind of internal deadline you've set yourself.

It's actually difficult to be committed to your project, to take action *and* be receptive and open to working with the flow of energy as it comes. *Very Difficult.* It's important for me that I don't beat myself up about this when I can't do it perfectly. I need to stop, take a deep breath, and remember the two most important things.

The lesser important thing is that the outcome of the project doesn't matter. Only my growth as a soul in a body on this planet actually matters. That is my actual job description, not homeopath or flower essence practitioner or book author or partner with Nature.

The greater important thing is that my higher self is whole and perfect as it's always been since its creation. This wholeness *is.* Everything else is incidental.

FOLLOW YOUR BLISS: JOURNAL ENTRY, MAY 19, 2010

I sit on the lawn at Apple Valley Farm preparing to write in my journal. In my mind's eye, the trees around me become the palm trees of the Shamanic Valley Campground. A nearby outdoor bathtub becomes a hot spring pool. The crystal around my neck becomes the cluster of crystals at the head of the pool. This grass is the grass of the campground lawn. These chirping birds become the cawing ravens. Why have I returned to this place today? Yes, of course. Our writing teacher read us these words: "Follow your bliss."

The Shamanic Valley campground for me is a place of bliss, belonging, and connection. I feel myself energetically enter the earth and spread out until my shape becomes a thin layer beneath the whole of the campground area. Above me are the landing strip with its windsock for guiding small planes, the road to the upper springs, the hills that ring the campground where I walk with Skip at dawn, the spring beyond the single outhouse, the water flowing from the spring down through the small gully, the arrow weed bushes that ring the campground, the main road coming in, the double outhouse with its two rooms named for men and for women, the grassy lawn with palms where the ravens and bats rest, the dishwashing area, the fire circle with its benches, the picnic tables with the nearby book cupboard, the bathing area with its shower and tub, and lastly, the pit of the source water with its two soaking pool outflows. I'm spread out underneath all of it, encircling it, embracing it with my energy. I send the campground and the surrounding desert a message from my heart, "I love you, I know you, I will return."

At this campground there was a moment of following my bliss. I let my world be rocked by the book *Co-Creative Science* by Machaelle Small Wright. This is where I originally connected to Nature and said, "I want to learn from you. Will you enroll me in your curriculum?" Speaking these words yourself, if you are earnest and speaking from your heart, will evoke a response from Nature that is beyond amazing. These words change the course of your destiny. They are that powerful. You begin living a new life where work, learning, and joy are one. Forget boredom, it will never darken your door again. You will be launched on a great journey, and like Christopher Columbus, you will discover new realms.

One of the greatest joys for me is that I get to do things that feel important. I have assignments, real responsibilities that feel substantial and meaningful. Even if I feel tired at the end of the day, it's a satisfied tired. I feel as though I'm saturated with something that feeds a deep need and satisfies a yearning in my core.

I'm still under the ground, healing the earth here. I send blessings to the campground host, that he be happy and protected. I send blessings to all the people and animals that come here, that they be happy and protected and that they have the capacity to comprehend and hold the sacredness of this place.

And now I'm leaving. I lift out of the ground and hover above the campground, looking down on the palm trees. I see the airstrip below and the road coming in and the road continuing on toward the upper springs. I lift up higher and see the western part of the United States and the Pacific Ocean down below me. I move to the north and come down until I see myself sitting on a chair at the Apple Valley Farm. And now I find myself all the way returned, completely here in just this one place. I take just one more moment to give thanks for the lovely journey to my favorite place.

FROM THE PWN HANDBOOK

It will be apparent by now that studying Nature's curriculum is not akin to studying an academic subject. There is very little reading involved. When you're working on a project with Nature, naturally you do all the research that would normally be required. I read books on the care of chickens before we started our flock, and books on beekeeping before we brought home our hives.

If you create a project in partnership with Nature, you will educate yourself on the area you're working in if it's new to you. However, these studies will be adjuncts to what you're really doing, which is conducting your project in partnership with Nature. Reading books and articles and talking with experts will help you ask the right questions, but they won't enable you to predict Nature's answers.

Nature often gives me answers that vary from the conventional wisdom of whatever field I'm working in. When that happens, I usually double check the answer, asking, "Is this really what you recommend?" If I get a clear yes, I take a deep breath and jump off into the unknown. This new step, because it is unconventional, will likely enlarge our knowledge of how to best work in whatever field is involved.

For this reason, I keep especially detailed records when a project veers into the unknown. If, for example, I'm advised to do something unusual in the garden, it may be months before I see the results. I need a way to track it so I can later evaluate why Nature offered those particular instructions.

Sometimes I will understand Nature's reasons when I see the results, and sometimes I won't. There are times when a sudden realization will strike me much later and I have an "aha" moment. Elements unclear before fall into place and I jump up to a new level of realization. There are times when I can see previously unperceived patterns by looking back over my records. Either way, keeping careful records on each project is an important part of the research you do as a student of Nature's curriculum. You may find that you are working on the frontier of your subject. When this happens, you take part in uplifting your discipline, expanding it into what it must become to satisfy the needs of our time.

As you continue to work with Nature, and as you gain experience, you'll find that your projects become more complex. As in conventional learning, you master the fundamentals before moving on to more advanced material. Nature is continually evaluating your response to challenges in order to assess what material to present next. This evaluation is not like a grade in school. There is no wrong or right in Nature's school. You learn by doing and you progress at your own pace. The questions you ask Nature are one gauge of how well you've integrated your experiences. If you can ask a clear question about something, it shows Nature that the concept involved is formulated to some extent in your conscious mind. You will then be given work that develops your experience in that concept. If it's something that you're just sensing, but it's vague and you can't ask about it clearly, Nature will offer other, more fundamental work until you're ready.

Because Nature responds to your timing, it's not possible to know how your curriculum will unfold over time. For example, I've been growing and creating flower essences. Nature has guided me through this project, telling me which flowers to grow and giving me the exact process for making the essences. We've also been working on a label to use for half-ounce dropper bottles. I'm aware that we'll be creating essence blends, but I don't yet know the recipes for the blends or how they'll be packaged. I also don't have the design for the website, or the description of each essence. I just have to trust that we'll be able to navigate those steps at the right time. Much of the time, I'm forging ahead into the unknown in this way, without a clear chart of where I'm going. Nature may have a better overview than me, but Nature also doesn't have a predetermined timeline.

Nature doesn't know when the project will be complete, or even if it will be completed. Nature can't let me know what to expect ahead of time, because much depends on how I learn and grow, and also on how our project is affected by events in the world around us. For these reasons, Nature mostly just shows me the next step in the process, and I have to take the rest on faith.

REMAKING OUR WORLD:
JOURNAL ENTRY, JUNE 16, 2010

The reality of things unseen. Uploading my writings to a blog—even an anonymous blog—commits me to a public avowal of a belief in things unseen: energy vortices, underground cities, ley lines, Lemurian temples. Compared to these, homeopathy seems rather staid and pedestrian. I present the blog posts as stories so that more people can read and enjoy them. But there are things unseen in the stories, too, unseen assumptions about how the world works that are different from what is generally accepted in our society. We know, at least theoretically, that everything is created from energy. The unseen link, which some are aware of, and most are not, is that energy is created from thought and aspiration. Therefore, energy follows thought and aspiration, and can be moved by thought and aspiration.

The pictures of the Deepwater Horizon oil spill in the Gulf of Mexico are horrifying, and they are intended to be so. It is humanity's thought and intention to show ourselves in a visceral way a normally hidden side of our petroleum lifestyle. Many people and species of the Gulf have agreed on a soul level to sacrifice so that we might see this, and be compelled to make another choice in our means of transportation. This is human thought and aspiration in action, remaking our world.

To the waters, plants, and animals of the Gulf, Dr. Masaru Emoto, author of *The Hidden Messages in Water,* suggests we say, "Please forgive me. I apologize. Thank you. I love you."

It is right that each of us apologize, because we each have

participated in our chosen lifestyle that includes the use of petroleum for our transportation and our casual acceptance of corporate control of many aspects of our daily lives. It is right that we ask forgiveness for allowing things to get to the point that this sacrifice is necessary. It is right that we thank the water and living beings of the Gulf for their willingness to make that sacrifice. And it is right that we send them love and healing from the deepest well of our open hearts.

Now we wait. More Earth changes are coming. More sacrifices will be made so that we will see the implications of our choices. And so that it will become easier to make new choices than to remain the same. I want to enfold the quiet beauty of this day in my heart and carry it like a talisman to protect my spirit from becoming overwhelmed by chaos in the days to come. May it help me remember that it is my thoughts and human aspirations in alignment with the thoughts and aspirations of millions of others that are creating these Earth changes for the benefit of us all.

LUNAR ECLIPSE, JUNE 26, 2010

I have my alarm set for 4:18 a.m. in order to be awake and watching the fullest part of the lunar eclipse at 4:38. I'm dreaming. In my dream, Ursa is conducting a class. She tells me to go get a warm washcloth and something else—I can't remember what. These items are clearly to comfort me with the implication that she is going to give me some difficult news about something personal to me.

Suddenly I experience a tremendous surge of energy rushing up and through my entire body. This surge is similar to a surge I experienced on the morning of April 25, the day before we opened a vortex on the Sutter Buttes. With the surge, I wake up. It is shortly after 4 a.m. I go on our deck and get in the hot tub. The eclipse is in process. I bathe myself in the energy of the eclipse until shortly after dawn, around 5:00 a.m. During that time, the veil between dimensions is thin in general, and I see a couple of things in particular that are not from our third-dimensional reality.

The first is a triangular black shape that moves fast and low horizontally across my field of vision. It is above the ground, higher than the nearby tall bushes, but not as high as the tops of the pine trees. It is larger than the largest birds here, larger than a turkey vulture or a bald eagle, and also moves too rapidly to be a bird. It is too small and low to be a plane. It is maybe the size of a large kite, but moves too quickly to be a kite, and it is too low and too close to me.

The other unusual thing I see is a flash of light that seems to occur in front of me and to my left. I say "seems to occur" because I don't see the flash itself; rather I see the leaves of the nearby tall bushes light up as if an intense light source has suddenly flared on them. It looks like a sudden flash of lightning, without seeing lightning or hearing thunder; and the sky is completely clear.

I imagine we'll see the effect of the eclipse energy ripple outward as we move through the summer.

CO-CREATIVE PARTNERSHIP:
JOURNAL ENTRY, JUNE 30, 2010

We are pushing against the barriers of earthly understanding, the barriers that protect us from experiencing all that is, so that we may conduct our lives within the time-space limits of earthly life. We have chosen to live within those limits because they are what make life on Earth unique and such a great school. This great school has been like a high school. We study, learn, and grow, but eventually high school ends and it's time to move on to a larger, wider, and deeper school. In our expanded school of college or the work world, we continue to learn and grow. So it is that we on Earth have come to graduation. It is time to leave the smaller school that life on Earth has been until now and matriculate into a more expanded school.

What about time-space limits? They will still be prominent features of our earthly life. A century after acquiring theoretical knowledge of it, we will actually be embracing the realization that time and space are relative, and making this knowledge our own. Like riding a roller coaster, this will be both scary and fun. If you like adventures, you'll love the ride. We'll know that we can have more bodies, more lifetimes, more power of intention, and more ability to create our world. To be a victim now means struggle. Hopefully the strugglers can join our new school's introductory curriculum.

One of the first assignments of our new school will be to learn more about how our intention creates form. It is the soul that intends, but intention is only part of creation. The soul alone cannot clothe our intention in form. The time has come for humans and Nature to work together in co-creative partnership in accordance with the grand design for our universe.

A MAGICAL BOY: JOURNAL ENTRY, JULY 22, 2010

Dickon. In my journal, I call him Dickon after the magical boy in *The Secret Garden* by Frances Hodgson Burnett. In the book, nature shares all its secrets with Dickon. A fox sits on his shoulder and a crow flies beside him, accompanying him on his journeys over the moor. Dickon tells his friend Mary that he will keep her secret safe, just as he keeps safe the location of every bird's nest on the moor.

In real life, the boy I call Dickon is my son, and he is a magical boy, although at 25 "young man" would be a more accurate term. Like Dickon in *The Secret Garden*, animals are drawn to him. As a boy, our cat would sleep on the top of his head. I would have pushed the cat aside, but Dickon just let her sleep there. Our dog managed to somehow to spend more time in Dickon's bed than in any other.

Being Dickon's mom was enough to give me gray hairs at 40. Dickon is a born peacemaker and will not engage in any type of conflict. You can try to goad him, rant and rave, or tie yourself in knots, but he will not engage you in conflict whatever you do. I have sometimes been called stubborn, but I readily acknowledge that I have met my master in the arena of stubbornness, and his name is Dickon. Now you may think, *Okay, this is good. He won't fight, he won't argue, what could be better?* But that's because you think that if he doesn't argue, he's docile, that he does as he should. Oh no, I didn't say that! He does precisely what he wants, and he doesn't argue about it, end of story.

And one of the things he wanted as a teenager was to sleep late. Another was to take a long shower in the morning. The fact that he was enrolled in a high school two bus rides across town didn't change the fact that he wanted to sleep late, take a long shower, and take his time. Did you know that some kids consider the prospect of expulsion from school to be an inducement? That's quite a divergent mindset from my own schoolgirl thinking that led to nearly straight As and a college scholarship.

As a parent, I did my ineffectual best to comply with the laws of our state and get my child to school every day on time. I'd knock on his bedroom door in the morning, although he had a perfectly working alarm clock. I'd turn off the hot water at the water heater to get him out of the shower. I even occasionally drove him to meet the second bus when he'd missed the first one. And when the school threatened me with citation, I told them that he was bigger than me and stronger than me, and that I couldn't make him do anything.

Now that you know how obstinate my son can be, maybe you're thinking he's a bit of an unpleasant person. But no, actually, he's a magical young man. His magic is partly in his sweetness, his calmness, and his deep there-ness that's so soothing. People as well as animals like to be around this man of few words. The words he does say are finely chiseled, like minimalist poetry. His drawings are like his words: spare. Just a few lines, maybe the contour of a face and a smile, bring out a wealth of expression.

Sometimes people tell me that Dickon won't talk to them. I tell them that Dickon refuses to chitchat. He will only talk if one or both of you is passionate about the subject. He certainly won't talk for your convenience or to fill up space.

Here's a hint: To engage his passion, talk about music. One time a psychic tuned in to him, just knowing his name, his age, and that he was my son. She said, "Oh, my! Music is flowing from his soul."

Yes, I thought, *beautiful music from a beautiful soul.*

It has been one of the privileges of my life to be Dickon's mother and to give him some of the love and support he needed as a child. I spent many hours reading him stories and later listening to stories of his invention. I still have maps of enchanted lands that he created. I always made sure that he had his own room because his soul required solitude, even if that room was just a big walk-in closet converted into a bedroom. He never needed much space, but he needed time alone. As an adult, he's been living within the expansive vibration of a variety of tree-filled natural environments. Each one has been a magical and fitting place for a magical young man.

MASTERY: JOURNAL ENTRY, JULY 22, 2010

Mastery. This word was spoken today and I felt it resonate within my expanded self. To know an art or a science takes time, intention, and determination. Some months ago the word *mastery* occurred within me and challenged me to own it. Homeopathy is wide and deep. So wide and so deep, in fact, that one can spend a lifetime of study and practice and never completely master its beguiling ways. How could one think of mastering such a discipline?

Yet at some point in the journey, you arrive at a way stop that is at least the beginning of mastery. I am no longer a neophyte homeopath. I am no longer an infatuated lover entranced by the beauty and power of this craft. I know what I'm doing. I even know what to do when I make the inevitable mistakes that lead to new learning.

I have come to this place of knowing through intention, strength, and determination, and now it is mine to own. And I own it by saying, "I am a master of the practice of homeopathy." By saying this, I accept and own what has already happened. Greater knowledge, understanding, and intuition have combined with the unfolding of my spiritual self in such a way that I, the practitioner, although still learning, am practicing from a deeper, richer space. I know the practice of homeopathy, I have mastered it.

Imagine a magical coin. On one side, in beautiful calligraphy is inscribed: "*Intention.*" On the other, in bold Times Roman, is inscribed: "**Determination.**" The coin as a whole stands for one thing with two sides: intention and determination. Perhaps that one thing is resolve. Resolve is the genesis. My soul created a resolution. To enact the resolution, I activated the intention: I want to heal. That is, I want to transmit healing and I want others to accept healing as a result.

I activated the intention first, because intention always comes before manifestation. Once the intention is activated clearly and fully, determination must also be activated to carry me through the lifetimes of learning that will follow. Intention and determination must partner and balance each other. If intention flags, I will be fruitlessly busy, doing things without purpose or coherence. If determination flags, I will mire in inertia. When they work hand in hand, I surf effortlessly to the shores of my higher desire.

On the X

CHAPTER 4

MIMZY REDUX

We are three soul sisters on a mission, Sybil, Claire, and me. It's July 25, 2010, and four months have passed since the Mimzy Project. Now the snow in the high vastness on the backside of Mount Shasta has melted, and we can physically perform the ceremony at Medicine Lake that the Mimzy tethers did energetically last April.

I am driving Sybil's car and we are approaching Jolly Point, a place that is dear to me because of the lightheartedness that enters into me when I'm here. The logical, linear world drops away and I enter a garden of connectedness and inner knowing. We are talking to Kalia on the phone, which is enough in itself to bump my consciousness up a notch or two. But the approach of this special place is even more intense. My heart is pounding with such excitement that focusing on driving becomes more difficult.

I park in the lot and run to the spot that is the energetic launching point for my connection to the vortices of Mount Shasta. I touch the sacred, but ordinary-looking tree stump and Manzanita bush that are the totems of this place. They welcome my return as my heart opens to the deep satisfaction of being in a place of complete rightness. Quickly, I connect to the other points and send a special greeting to those within the mountain. They are aware of my presence and are also sending me greetings of love and connectedness.

I don't linger long. We must set up a camp on the shores of Medicine Lake before dark.

When we reach Medicine Lake, we don't find the right campsite immediately. To best do our work, we will need one located on the lake's edge. Sybil is sure that one has been energetically set aside for us. So we work through a process of trial and error, logic and intuition, until we find it. It's a lovely large site with a picnic table and level tent sites, away from the distraction of the road and right on the water.

After setting up camp, we face another unknown. When is our work to be done? Late night? Early morning? Or some other time? Late night turns out not to feel right, so we go to sleep. In the middle of the night, I awaken with the knowledge that the time has come. I'm drowsy with sleep and don't really feel like getting out of my cozy sleeping bag. Yet I hear Claire moving around. She's awake and out of her tent. The inner urging that "now is the time" is insistent.

I get up and ask Claire to get the crystals. I wake Sybil gently—she's deeply asleep. The words are put into my mouth to say: "The Mimzys are waiting for us." Later, Sybil tells me that only those words could have gotten her up.

I can't tell you the exact content of our ceremony. Such moments are indescribable anyway. I can tell you that the moon's reflection in the ripples of the lake played energetic games with us, heightening our consciousness and sense of connectedness with all that is. And I can tell you that the Mimzy beings used me to request of Sybil that she say a special prayer in Japanese called the Matsu prayer. I say,

"They used me," because it was clearly not something I would have thought of myself. This prayer shifted the energy and stabilized our work, making our newly formed vortex stronger and more durable.

PANTHER MEADOWS

In the morning, we drive to Panther Meadows on Mount Shasta. We again play the "find the right campsite" game. An easier challenge in this case. After setting up tents, we hike to the sacred spring. We sit near the spring in silent meditation along with several other pilgrims who have been drawn to this storied place. I connect effortlessly to Saint Germain, the guardian of this meadow. The veils are very thin here; the connection is easy and strong.

I ask Claire to pass me our bag of crystals. I hold the bag in my two hands, asking the saint to infuse the crystals with his vibration. My hands gradually become warmer until they are hot. It's much more heat than I have ever experienced when doing healing work. I send gratitude to Saint Germain for granting my request and for giving me this direct, and to me undeniable, evidence of his presence. Because, after all, the work we are doing, and how we perceive it, would not seem sane to most people.

Sometimes you question yourself. "Is this real, or am I merely making it up in my own mind?" And yes, I know it's possible to use your mind to create the sensation of heat in your hands. So my experience would prove nothing to a skeptic. But it is helpful to me because I know that I ordinarily don't have the ability to make my hands heat up. It only happens when I'm aware of a connection to something greater than my earthly self, and when I have an intention to send energy using a power greater than my earthly self. The heat in my hands validates that I am connected to a greater spirit that is working through me for the success of our project.

Later that day we meditate and perform a ceremony in the meadow. At the end of our meditation, I energetically infuse one of the crystals with my love and toss it into a small rivulet of water.

The day is one of delight and relaxation for us. The next day we will drive to Crater Lake.

CRATER LAKE

Crater Lake astounds us with its eye-popping beauty. I've been here twice before, but memory doesn't prepare me for the tremendous jolt of energy that runs up my spine when I first see it again.

Our driving destination is a vista point with a large parking lot on the west side of the lake. It overlooks an island floating in the incomparable blue-greenness of the lake. The overcast grayness of the sky adds a touch of subtlety to the colors. Our hiking destination can be seen from the parking lot: the Watchman Lookout Station standing like a sentinel on the highest point above the lake.

The path to the lookout tower is a short seven-tenths of a mile long, but it takes about 40 minutes to traverse its cascade of switchbacks. Once there, the place is crowded. Too crowded, we feel, to start our work. The lookout tower is closed, but adjacent to it is a large stone parapet overlooking the lake. From this vantage point, we can clearly see dozens of mountains and several lakes in the sweeping landscape below. A large sign graphically reproduces the view and helpfully names each mountain and lake. We can see Mount Shasta,

Klamath Lake, and Bird Heaven.

We are waiting for people to leave, but they seem to be staying, possibly to wait out the rain that is now arriving. We decide that each of us will find a place suited to her unique energy, and each of us will begin the ceremony within herself.

I choose the top of a high group of rocks, the highest point on the stone parapet, and begin sending energy to each of our other Mimzy vortices around Mount Shasta and also to the Sutter Buttes. I connect each point back to our new vortex, the place where I'm now sitting. I gather energy and send it on a scythe-shaped trajectory from Crater Lake to Klamath Lake, then down to Bird Heaven and curving around to Mount Shasta, the Mother Herself.

I'm not aware of where Claire and Sybil are, but after a time I notice that the other people have all left and Sybil is chanting her Matsu prayer aloud. The sky is much darker and there is lightning not too great a distance away. Sybil finishes her timeless prayer and joins me on the high rock. Each of us sends her essence into a crystal and buries it there at this high spot.

As soon as we complete the burying of the crystals, the electromagnetic dynamics of the place instantly change. A bolt of lightning hits a nearby lightning rod, crackles the air, and throws Sybil backward. She hits her head on a boulder. Claire's fine straight hair is standing straight upward. I wonder how much of a charge Saint Germain put in those crystals!

We hastily decide that it's time to leave. We quickly descend, stopping only to snap a few pictures and for Claire to bury one last crystal where it wants to be: at the end of a switchback near a profusion of flowers and overlooking the lake.

As we descend, we're filled with joy and a sense of accomplishment. We've done everything we were asked to do, and now we bask in a celebratory feeling. It seems as though the Mimzy beings are celebrating with us. We can almost hear them popping champagne corks.

We decide that a motel in town actually sounds better than setting up camp in the rain. So we three soul sisters end our day freshly showered, in clean nightclothes, and in soft beds with warm and grateful hearts.

The next day, we meet Skidmore and our dog Skip at a nearby restaurant, as we have previously arranged. Skip is ecstatic to see me after a three-day absence. After our meal, Skidmore, Skip, and I leave in our small RV, while Claire and Sybil return home.

Skidmore and I then spend several days traveling in a large loop, tracing a route that I will retrace six weeks later with Sky. On this trip, I connect each mountain and lake we visit to the Mimzy energy grid. Later I realize that I have reprised my role as a scout, preparing the way for the work that Sky and I will soon do.

Sacred Work

Shortly after our return home, I receive an email from Martha, who was a participant in the Mimzy Project. She lives in my area, and writes to say that Zara will soon visit and will be scheduling healing sessions for those that want them. I sign up for a healing session, little realizing that my life is about to take another turn.

As I'm about to leave the house on the day of my session, a crystal on my nightstand seems to call to me and I put it in my pocket. Once at the session, Zara and I greet each other.

Join the Conversation

As you work with Nature, you may have experiences that you'd like to share with others. Please join the conversation on the Partnering with Nature website. You can go to www. MaureenShepard.com and select "Partnering with Nature" or visit www.PartneringWithNature.com. Comment and "like" us on the Partnering with Nature Facebook page (www. facebook.com/PartneringWithNature).

We don't know one another well; we've just seen each other at two large gatherings during the Mimzy Project. Zara puts me on a massage table and begins to work on what I assume are acupressure points on my body. I soon become aware that something unusual is happening. The energy shifts and becomes more intense.

Zara is receiving a download of information about my work and our soul relationship. She tells me that I am to grow flowers and make flower essences. She says that new flowers will be coming to the planet and that I am to make essences of them. She tells me that this is sacred work. These things I can comprehend, even though they are amazing and completely unexpected. She also makes mention of some things that I can't even grasp, something about a violet ray and another star system.

Later Zara told me she saw petals and stamens floating in the atmosphere. They were seeded by birds, nature spirits, and other sentient life forms, and carried by bees and wind. She knew that I would be one of the people who would know how to use the plants as medicines.

The session was profoundly moving to both of us. We both felt grateful for the grace of spirit that had established a connection between us. Zara advised me to sit in the garden for a few moments before leaving and to write whatever came to me.

Here is what I wrote.

ESSENCES OF FLOWERS:
JOURNAL ENTRY, AUGUST 7, 2010

You were shown flowers and given scents of flowers for a reason: so that you will know that what Zara spoke of—your work with plants, water, and flower essences—is true. This is your path—one of your many paths—to self-realization and connection with your true self and with all that is. The red flower with daisy-like petals and thick black stamens grows beside a pond, where someday you may find it and ask it for permission to infuse its essence for the healing of others.

New flowers from Venus and other places will soon be growing here. Make essences from these flowers. The use of flower essences in ley-line work can be even more powerful than the use of crystals. The crystal in your pocket has been connected to all the Mimzy points. Now plants from those areas will start talking to you.

> *Deva of plants, Deva of flowers, Deva of water,*
> *Teach me your ways.*
> *I will serve you.*
> *Allow me to bring your knowledge of healing to*
> *humankind.*

ESALEN

We drop Laurel's daughters off at school and take the famous Pacific Coast Highway south. Laurel is a friend and a student of shamanism. Weeks before, when planning this day, we talked of hunting for stones at one of three places: on a nearby beach, on the coastal highway, or at some property that her neighbor knew about. At the time, the idea of the coastal highway had pulled at me, but since things sometimes evolve differently than I expect, all had been left open. It was understood that we would be using guidance and feeling our way.

The previous evening, I had used the Google Earth

software to locate a point that called to me. I "saw" us finding stones there. That morning, Laurel told me that she, too, had received the understanding that we were to go down the coastal highway, and that we were to do earth energy work there.

As we enter the intense energy that pervades the dramatic coastal cliff area, I locate the point I had identified the night before on Laurel's dashboard GPS map. When we reach that point, Laurel feels we should continue further, so we drive on. We reach the world-famous Esalen Institute at Big Sur, which has been a force in the human potential movement for nearly 50 years. We drive in and ask if there is any way we can see the place, but are told we must be signed up for a workshop, seminar, or at least a massage to use the grounds. So we continue driving south.

After a time, Laurel senses that we've gone far enough, that there is something further ahead for her to see or do, but not today. So we turn around. I locate a new point on the GPS where I sense we should stop. Laurel comments that my new point must be somewhere near Esalen. As we approach the point, I remember that Kalia has told me to look for signs in nature. So I tell Laurel to look for something unusual, like a raven or a rainbow.

When we reach the point, there is a pull-over on the ocean side of the road, so I ask Laurel to stop. I get out of the car and I sense that I'm to move to my left and closer to the cliffs. That's when I see it. There is a large, white X nailed to the ground. I think, *They're making it easy for me again.* I walk up a short incline opposite the X and I'm standing on the cliff overlooking the ocean. This is obviously where we are to do our earth-energy work. I tell Laurel that this is it, and it's a lesson to me that the signs don't always have to be from the natural world. Clearly a manmade X will do.

Laurel brings her mesa, or shamanic bundle of power stones and crystals. She spreads the mesa cloth to create an altar, and then uses her tiny rattle to call in the six directions. I'm connected to the Deva of the Mimzy Project and my Nature spirit and White Brotherhood guides. I connect to the Mimzy points: Jolly Point, Lake Siskiyou, Lake Shastina, Rumbling Point, Bird Heaven, and Medicine Lake; and to additional points at the Sutter Buttes and Crater Lake. I connect to Telos and I'm laughing as I send love and greetings there. I also connect to three points I had visited in my trip with Skidmore a few weeks before: Mount Hood, Mount Saint Helens, and Mount Jefferson.

Once I have all these connections open and connected to my current position, I gather them all in a ball and throw the ball to Serpent Mound, a vortex in the Midwest that is under Kalia's protection, connecting them there. I ask and intend that all these connections stabilize this place, and that this place be strongly connected to the global grid. Finally, Laurel closes the directions, and it is done.

Then I use my flower essences to balance and stabilize our process. Waves of happiness and satisfaction wash over us. We feel our work to be rightly completed and it is good.

Back in the car, we begin driving northward. It turns out that our vortex is only 500 to 600 feet from the entrance to Esalen. We had thought that the work was not only for this area of the coastal cliffs, but was specifically intended to protect and stabilize Esalen. When we see how close the vortex is, this conclusion seems even more probable.

As we drive northward, I again locate on the GPS the spot

for finding stones that I had identified the night before on Google Earth. As the car reaches that place, there is a white car backing up slowly across the road at a 90-degree angle to us, temporarily blocking the road. We slow down, and I feel that this is a sign that we are to stop here. Laurel drives into a pull-over on the right and we get out to explore, but the energy is all wrong. In the meantime, the white car has turned down a narrow road on the other side of the highway. Laurel says we need to follow the car. We do so and find that we are on a road to a place called Pfeiffer Beach.

At the beach, we pay a day-use fee, park and walk onto the beach and up to a high vantage point above the water and boulders below. We eat our lunch, enjoying the magnificent view. As we descend, we look for stones. I select a gnome-like one and one that is red and heart-shaped with a piece chipped out of it—a broken heart. Laurel also finds stones that are right for her. As we leave the beach, fog is beginning to roll in. The return drive is stunningly beautiful and we drive it feeling gratitude for this day.

Orbs among the flowers

CHAPTER 5

SKY TOUR

It's September 2010. Sky is here and we are setting out on an 11-day tour to do earth-energy work. Our itinerary is not entirely determined. We know that we must go to Panther Meadows and Medicine Lake, but otherwise we will follow the guidance of spirit as it unfolds.

PANTHER MEADOWS

We drive to Panther Meadows and set up camp near a field of iridescent violet and fuchsia wildflowers. Then we drive up the mountain to the end of the road. I take the crystals that want to come with me. Sky takes her crystal singing bowl for creating healing sound. We both see the place to go, a vibrant green patch of low-growing foliage that beckons us up the mountain slope.

As we climb to the place, I'm singing an old song from my Girl Scout days, "White Coral Bells." I'm weeping, although I don't know why. But I'm sure that this song is somehow a message to us.

White coral bells
Upon a slender stalk.

Lilies of the Valley deck my garden walk.
Oh, don't you wish
That you could hear them ring?
That will happen only
When the fairies sing.

When we reach the spot, a lovely aroma envelops us. The low foliage is actually some kind of pine exuding a heavenly scent. We sit on boulders and put our crystals on a lovely red cloth Sky has brought for just such an occasion. From this place we can see the bank of Lake Siskiyou far below.

We're about to start our ceremony when we're joined by a young man who appears to be in his early 20s. Sky starts the bowl singing and I connect up this place with all the other Mimzy points plus Crater Lake, the Sutter Buttes, and the vortex at Big Sur. I ask and intend that this grounding be used for my highest good and the good of all on Earth.

The energy of this ceremony is high, intense, and pure. When Sky is finished playing, the three of us each take a crystal, infuse it with our essence, and throw it into the mass of vibrant green foliage. The young man leaves us, and Sky and I linger on the rocks enjoying the feeling. Another man joins us and thanks Sky for the crystal bowl music, which had fortuitously started as his group was infusing energy into some crystals.

When we return to the parking lot, I balance the energy work with soil balancers and stabilize it with flower essences. At first, I'm only able to identify one of the essences, although I know that two are needed. Sky feels a shift in energy each time I say the name of the Moon essence, and finally she realizes that I need her help. So we get it done.

We get in the car and drive the short distance down to a parking lot for Panther Meadows. We're hiking the trail to the sacred springs when we run into Zara and her daughter returning from the meadow. On greeting Zara, my energy surges higher. She immediately asks me if I'm doing flower-essence work and comments that the flowers are blooming much later this year than usual. I assume she's indicating that flower essences can still be made at this time, even though it would usually be too late in the season.

At the spring, I hold the crystals in my hands as on my previous visit, and ask Saint Germain to infuse his essence into them. This time, my hands become nicely warm, though not as dramatically hot as before. As I meditate, I see roads, cliffs, bridges, and waterfalls. I see Sky and myself at all these places.

I also decide to make a flower essence from the flowers growing near our campsite. Sky feels that those flowers magnetically pulled her to want that particular site. They called to Sky and now they're calling to me.

FIRST ESSENCE

That night, I don't sleep much. There's too much energy running through my body. I'm shivering as if with cold, but it's probably more energy than cold. On waking, I begin to make the flower essence. I test that I need 14 of the small flowers I see around me. I am told to gather the more violet ones, which are a deeper color than the fuchsia ones. I use only the petals, not the stalk, leaves, or stamens. The stamens are difficult to remove, but I manage it using the tweezers on my pocketknife.

I float the petals I've collected on water in a white ceramic dish because we have no glass. After it absorbs the sun for one and a quarter hours, I remove the petals with my tweezers and pour the essence into a plastic bottle, then lay the bottle next to my large crystal for another hour and a quarter to stabilize it. The camp host says the flowers I've gathered are called *slender penstemons.*

The camp host suggests to me that we look for what he calls *cosmic lilies* on the path to the higher meadows. Sky and I set out to look for them, Sky carrying her crystal bowl. We hike quite a way without finding the lilies we're seeking. After a time, we find a bare, tall, spirally twisted stump standing near the path like an obelisk. A thin, bare, horizontally bent tree stands nearby. Sky says this indicates an energy portal.

I hike maybe 50 feet farther up the path and find a large stump embedded in a rounded mound. I call to Sky that I'm to stay with this stump during our time here. Sky sits in a split between the twisted tree and one growing next to it, and plays her bowl. The sound infuses the space between us, filling the huge portal that appears to be here. Again I see images of our trip in my third eye.

After our enchanting concert, we hike back to Sky's car and drive to the natural foods grocery in the City of Mount Shasta. There we have lunch. At Sky's suggestion, we buy a chocolate cookie "for the fairies." I also buy two airplane-sized containers of brandy to preserve the flower essence. Then we drive to Lake Siskiyou, park, and walk to the place where we had opened a portal last April.

We are on the same bank that we had seen from high on the mountain the day before. Here Sky plays her bowl and we both throw infused crystals into the lake. I find a small stone that seems to have entities enfolded in it, and I take it with me, putting it in a bag with the rest of my stones and crystals.

The drive back to Panther Meadows is profound. We enter a slower, more vibrant reality. We pass the trees that frame the road as if in slow motion. It seems as if they are allowing us to experience their stately sense of time and place.

That evening, as we're walking to our campsite, Zara calls. Sky tells her that I made a flower essence. Zara says that makes her day. She says that this is sacred work, and that I will be bringing in flowers from the higher dimensions. I feel filled with gratitude that such work will be mine to do.

Back at the campsite, it's growing dark. Sky breaks the large chocolate cookie into three pieces and puts them in three different spots among a patch of slender penstemons. She takes a picture of the flower patch. In this photo, everything looks normal. A few minutes later, she takes another picture. This time several orbs of light are clearly visible in the photo. Sky says the orbs show that the fairies are here and that they are attracted to the cookie.

That night, I sleep soundly except for walking to the outhouse and back at about 3 a.m. The stars are stunningly gorgeous. I also read a few pages of the book *Behaving as if the God in All Life Mattered*. In these pages, Machaelle Small Wright explains that the devic realm creates a blueprint for a person's body based on the direction, purpose, and life contract of his or her soul. The Nature spirit realm manifests a body for the soul according to the blueprint. As long as a person is fulfilling his or her soul contract, the body is healthy because it has been constructed to be in balance for that direction and purpose.

Conversely, when a person uses his or her free will to make choices aligned with a different direction and purpose, ill health results because the body hasn't been constructed for those life choices.

MEDICINE LAKE

The next day, Sky and I return to the end of the road near the top of the mountain where we had performed the ceremony two days earlier. Sky takes a rock and a special crystal and goes into some trees to commune with the mountain. I hold the space for her by walking a nearby labyrinth. On the drive down the mountain, we again experience the sense of slow-motion time and the sense that the trees are sentinels honoring us on our departure.

We drive toward Medicine Lake. We reach Jolly Point and find the stump and see some of the lapis lazuli stones that our group left there in April. I had told Sky about an area near Jolly Point where there are tree stumps left standing after logging and a sense of sadness. I show her this place, and she feels it, too. The trees are experiencing the aftermath of some kind of abuse or trauma.

We go back to the car and get my flower essences and the Perelandra Soil Balancing Kit and Sky's crystal bowl, then we return to the place. Sky begins playing her bowl like a temple gong, tapping it rather than ringing it by circling the rim. I begin clearing the area using the Perelandra energy cleansing process. Then I balance and stabilize the process with the soil balancers and the flower essences. Sky continues to play as I do the Perelandra battle energy release process and the balancing and stabilizing for that. We leave with a clear sense that we've cleaned the energy at that place.

At Medicine Lake we find a campsite without good, level

tent spaces. On the beach we find a large circle of stones with relatively level sand inside of it, large enough for us both to sleep there. So we decide we'll ditch the tents for the night and sleep under the stars near the water and within that circle.

That night, after our dinner, we come to the circle and get in our sleeping bags. Sky brings out her bowl. The moon is above and directly in front of us. The waves on the lake have been choppy. Now the wind disappears and the lake becomes calm and the waters quiet. Sky begins playing. I notice three long, thin, white horizontal lines like long, thin clouds above the lake to our right; also a diagonal long, thin cloud above the lake to our left. As Sky plays, the clouds move closer together and form a V with the moon between them. Later I describe this to Zara and she says that the "clouds" are spacecraft.

Sky tells me that the sound of her bowl is making the water more crystalline. As Dr. Masaru Emoto has shown in *The Hidden Messages in Water* and other books, the structure of water can be changed by sound as well as by words and emotions. Water that has been exposed to classical music such as Beethoven's Symphony No. 5 in C Minor or Tchaikovsky's score for the ballet *Swan Lake* creates beautiful crystals when frozen. In contrast, in Dr. Emoto's experiments, water exposed to heavy metal music is unable to form crystals at all. The healing sounds from Sky's crystal bowl may be changing the structure of the lake water, making it more crystalline.

The lake remains calm all night. It's quite cold and we're surprised to find a layer of frost on our sleeping bags in the morning.

REDWOOD NATIONAL PARK

We drive all day and spend the night in a motel. The next

morning, we drive to the Lady Bird Johnson Grove in Redwood National Park. We take our time walking a one-mile loop through the majestic ancient forest. Sky and I are enthralled with the deep serenity and quiet of this timeless place.

On leaving, we drive to a nearby day-use site on the beach. While using the restroom at the nearby campground, we run into a huge male elk. He makes a call that reminds us of the sounds we heard from the other side of Medicine Lake during our night there. We've been wondering what animals had made that wild indefinable sound. Later we see the elk standing next to the road scratching his huge antler on a tree trunk.

We drive through Crescent City on our way to Jedediah Smith Redwood State Park. The town is depressed, the energy low and heavy. We take the back way into the park. We only go a short distance before pulling over. Sky wants to play her bowl and direct the energy toward the town of Crescent City. I sit in the car and hold the space while she plays. Later she tells me that she asked the trees to send the energy to the town through their root systems and to direct it wherever it needs to go. We continue driving down a narrow road framed by magnificent trees. I realize that this is one of the visions I saw when Sky played her bowl near the top of Mount Shasta the first day of our trip.

At the park, we intend to walk a half-mile loop through the redwood forest, except that we somehow veer off the trail, so we walk more than half a mile. That night there is rain, so we stay at a motel near the mouth of the Rogue River.

OREGON CAVES NATIONAL MONUMENT
In the morning Sky wakes up from a dream in which she

envisioned a circular place in a grove of stately evergreen trees. In her waking life, she's seen a picture of it, and she knows where it is, but she's given up the thought of going there because it's too far from everything else. I remark that I had given up on the thought of going to Oregon Caves National Monument for the same reason. We decide to look on the Internet and see if we're correct in our estimations of those distances. We find that, yes, the circular place really is too far away. But the Oregon Caves are not. It also turns out that the caves are near the Oregon Vortex, a place so powerful that things look misaligned. We understand that we're to go to both the Caves and the Vortex.

We decide to go there directly using a small back country road that we can see on our map. However, we can't find the road and even Sky's GPS won't pull it up. Earlier that morning, a grocery store checker had told us that it would be fine to use that road. But now we stop at a convenience store and a milk delivery man tells me that it's too dangerous. So we start back toward Crescent City and Jedediah Smith Redwood State Park. As we pass some large, offshore boulders, Sky connects with some kind of energy and begins carrying the energy with her.

We know that tours of the main cave at Oregon Caves National Monument are given on the hour. We expected to make the 3 p.m. tour, but we're too late. Then the reservations lady tells me that they're adding an extra tour for a smaller group at 3:30.

In the cave, Sky finds that the energy she picked up offshore leaves her. Apparently it just needed to hitchhike to the cave with us. I connect to all the Mimzy points including the now-usual Big Sur, Sutter Buttes, and Crater Lake on the

West Coast, as well as Serpent Mound in the Midwest. This time there is a connection to some place beyond Earth as well. I assume that this is a connection that the Mimzys and/or the White Brotherhood want brought in.

The cave feels like it needs clearing. A lot of damage has been done to it through human use. Its energy needs to be cleaned and its vortex reawakened. We reach a place where there are extremely steep stairs going up to a higher room. The stairs traverse a passageway between a large lower room and a higher chamber. This passageway appears to be the center of a funneling energy that starts in the higher room and funnels down through the passageway into the lower room. All of the group except me and the ranger climb into the upper room. I ask the ranger if there is any place in the cave where the energy feels a bit different. He says, "Yes, right here on the stairs." He sometimes gets dizzy in this area.

I fill up the space with energy from the connections I'm holding. I ask and intend that these connections ground here. Later as we leave, I do a quick energy clearing of the entire cave, sending the stuck energy on to the next higher step in its evolution.

Outside the cave, I take a photo of Sky at the entrance. There are large milky-looking orbs all around her in the photo. She takes a picture of me. In that photo, there is one smaller, well-defined orb to my left. We take a picture of the same spot with neither of us standing there. There are no orbs in that picture.

Back at the car, I balance and stabilize the work we've done in the cave using flower essences.

That night we check into a motel for the third night in a row. Rain is predicted for two more days.

THE OREGON VORTEX

We drive to the Oregon Vortex. As we approach, I notice a strange sensation as if the energetic fabric of the area is fractured. It's as if an energetic fault line had split and one segment moved relative to the other. I start to have an unusual headache as if a long pin is piercing in one side of my head and out the other.

At the vortex, we decide not to take the tour because it would require too much time and we still have far to drive. We notice that the tree roots here are growing in unusual, twisted shapes. I tell the man running the place that people say this vortex is the midpoint of a ley line between Eight Dollar Mountain and Mount Scott, and that the ley line possibly extends to Easter Island in the South Pacific Ocean.

He says he's heard that before, and that it's been said that Machu Picchu is also on a ley line connected to this place.

I tell him that Eight Dollar Mountain and Mount Scott are two points of a triangle and that Mount Shasta is the third point. As I'm talking to him, my stomach is getting increasingly queasy. Finally, I say I have to get out of this place. Sky is okay here, but it makes me sick in the same way that toxic solvents sometimes have made me sick in the past.

CANNON BEACH

The next day, we drive to Falcon Point, near Cannon Beach. People and their dogs are frolicking on the beach. Since it had rained all the previous day, and for much of the last four days, Sky had asked for just half a day without rain for our time on Cannon Beach. Amazingly, it's not raining. After enjoying Falcon Point, we look for a way to get close to the famous Haystack Rock on Cannon Beach itself. We find beach access and park near a circular wooden deck with bench seats and a dramatic snag tree in the center. The snag looks as though it has a being in it facing the sea.

We walk on the beach enjoying the magnificent view. Finally we return to the car to get Sky's bowl. On the bench on the circular deck, Sky lays out an altar. I add a stone I found on this beach, and also a crystal that I had tried to give Sky the day before when she put a crystal in the river near the vortex. This crystal had jumped away and gotten lost somewhere in the car and we were unable to find it. Today it has reappeared and so I place it with the others.

Sky plays the bowl for a long time, while I call in all the Mimzy points. I ask and intend that this ceremony bring enlightened energy to our planet. Later, Sky tells me that she has made the same request. After our ceremony, we place my crystal plus one of Sky's in the snag.

We have a delicious lunch of salmon wraps and fruit—our reward. Also we buy good chocolate in a candy store. As we leave Cannon Beach it starts to sprinkle. Driving inland, we stop at a large waterfall, walking up to a high bridge for a better view.

Driving on, as we approach Cascade Locks, we see a large rainbow on the other side of the Columbia River. I tell Sky that this may indicate that our work is to be done on that side of the Bridge of the Gods. We cross the bridge for the first time and find the heritage marker. This is where we'll park to do our work in the morning.

That night, we sleep in a horse barn that belongs to a friend. The horses can't get into the part of the barn where we're sleeping, but we can hear them moving in the night. There is a violent storm with high winds and pelting rain most of the night. The weather gods have answered Sky's prayer, and apparently the delayed release is all the stronger.

THE BRIDGE OF THE GODS

The next morning, we have eggs and tea in a café in Stevenson, Washington, before setting out for the heritage marker. On the way, Sky is drawn to drive down a certain street and we find ourselves at a historic steamboat landing which juts out into the river like a pier. We walk out on the pier and find ourselves upstream from the Bridge of the Gods. The energy here is soft and enfolding. The river here flows into a somewhat circular shape and the soft energy seems to spin gently in this circle. We bask in the magnetic energy of this vortex awhile, and then we drive to the heritage marker.

Following a path into the trees that line the cliff above the river, we find a natural altar and I lay out three crystals pointing toward Mount Hood. I call in all the Mimzy points, Serpent Mound, Mount Hood, and the 12 East Coast points where Sky has done previous earth-energy work. I ground them all here, and ask and intend that this grounding bring greater strength and light to all, and that this water be purified and enlivened by this work. After we are done, I balance and stabilize the work with flower essences.

We drive slowly across the bridge. No cars are around us so we take our time. We notice an island down below and decide to go there. We find the island and park the car. An informational sign tells us that the Native Americans who live in the area believe there is a family connection between Mount Hood, Mount Saint Helens, and Mount Adams. So I add connections to Mount Saint Helens and Mount Adams into the energy we are carrying.

Sky carries her crystal bowl as we walk across a grassy area to the tip of the island nearest the bridge. There Sky sits on the grass and plays her bowl, while I sit with my back against a helpful tree and hold the space. Later Sky says that the water and the air took in the sound and absorbed it, and then diffused it out, dispersing it everywhere.

After leaving the island, I try to rejoin the highway going east. However, I can't find a way to do this and I'm forced onto the highway going west. I get off at the first exit to turn around. As I exit, a police car is stopping somewhat perpendicular to our approach. I instantly remember the incident of the police car slowing us down at the start of the Mimzy Project and the perpendicular car slowing Laurel and me at Big Sur. I know we're at the Bonneville Dam, so instead of turning left to rejoin the freeway, I turn right. We drive slowly around the different buildings and parking areas, sending blessings to each area.

When we feel that we have accomplished whatever our presence is intended to achieve, we leave the Bonneville Dam and proceed east. We drive around Mount Hood and take the highway toward Klamath Falls. We try several times to find comfortable lodging near the Crater Lake junctions, but are not able to do so. Finally, we realize that we are meant to go all the way to Klamath Falls, even though that will mean more circling back the next day.

CRATER LAKE AND BIRD HEAVEN

We drive to Crater Lake. I have promised Sky that Crater Lake will not disappoint, and I'm certain it won't. I awoke with an understanding of our route for today. We are to drive to the west around Crater Lake, climb to the Watchman Lookout, bring energy from there east past Mount Scott, then back to Klamath Falls, down the depressed business area, south, and then west to Bird Heaven and finally back to the motel in Klamath Falls, the whole time bringing high energy with us. Quite a working day.

Now we drive to the Watchman Lookout parking lot. I sort out the crystals that want to go with us. Sky carries her bowl and we begin climbing the switchbacks. When we reach the point where Claire had buried a crystal, I realize for the first time what the function of that crystal is. It gives a transitional energy to climbers at that point as they move between the softer energy of the parking lot and lower hill and the intense energy of the Watchman vortex.

Finally we are there. I place Sky's crystal bowl on top of the high rock where Sybil, Claire, and I had buried our crystals. The energy here is clear, intense, and strong, yet we are calm within it. The water below is also calm, sparkling with light and energy and impossibly blue. Across the lake we see Mount Scott, where we know is located another powerful vortex. The ley line through Mount Scott passes through the Oregon Vortex and out into the Pacific, possibly to Easter Island.

We take pictures and read the informational signs that tell about the geology and history of the area. We notice that there is a cloud-like ring around the sun and two long, thin "clouds" on each side of the sun, both pointing toward Klamath Falls and Bird Heaven.

I climb on top of the large rock next to Sky's bowl, waiting for the right time to show itself. We talk to a couple we meet there about their travels. From their words and how they present themselves, we become aware that they are awakening and growing in consciousness. In our conversation, we nudge them on a bit. Other people are here talking and taking pictures.

Finally only two parties are left: two young Asian-American women who seem to be a couple and a group of three young Asian-Americans. One young man from the second party has also climbed the rock and told his companions that he is "rooted here." The young couple move toward the exit path, yet they linger. I have already connected this spot with all the Mimzy points, Serpent Mound, Mount Scott, the Sutter Buttes, Big Sur, the mouth of the Rogue River, Cannon Beach, and the Bridge of the Gods. I decide that the party of three is supposed to be here for Sky's playing and that the couple will be either pushed out or drawn in when Sky begins.

I hand Sky the bowl and say, "These people are supposed to be here." She begins playing. With the sound, energy courses from my crown and spirals down my spine to my root chakra. I ground it and ask for upliftment for our planet. I use the sound to direct a soft, golden light out and down into the Klamath Basin, filling the entire Basin with light. When the light reaches Mount Shasta, she sends it on out to the entire planet and beyond. Sky stops circling the bowl, pauses, and begins tapping it like a gong.

After a time, she pauses again, then starts the circling anew. This time energy courses up from my root, spiraling up my spine and out my crown chakra. I offer it to the higher beings and dimensions above. Finally Sky stops and asks me to join her on a stone bench. She asks me to relate our journey, telling where we have gone. After I name each place, she strikes the bowl like a gong.

Here's my chant with asterisks representing the gong strikes.

*"We leave home." * "We travel to the top of Mount Shasta." * "We go to Panther Meadows." * "We go to Jolly Point." * "We go to Medicine Lake." * "We return to Jolly Point." * "We drive to the redwoods." * "We travel through the redwoods on back roads." * "We see an elk on the beach." * "We drive to the mouth of the Rogue River." * "We go to the Oregon Caves." * "We drive to the Oregon Vortex." * "We go to Cannon Beach." * "We go to the Bridge of the Gods." * "We spend the night near Cascade Locks." * "We return to the Bridge of the Gods." * "We drive around Mount Hood and south to Klamath Falls." * "We come to Crater Lake." * "Our spirit travels before us back to Klamath Falls." * "We go to Bird Heaven." * "We return to Klamath Falls." * "We go to Stewart Mineral Springs." * "We return home." ***

Our ceremony is ended and we bury two crystals at the top of the same rock where Sybil, Claire, and I buried three crystals before.

We descend to the car and drive around the rest of the lake. At one point, Sky tosses a crystal toward the lake. I do the same at a place overlooking some ancient rocks. At this point we are near Mount Scott and opposite the Watchman, so I'm leaving this crystal directly opposite those buried at the Watchman lookout.

We return to Klamath Falls. When we reach the northern exit for Business Highway 97, I'm confused about the route and decide to drive that part of our route when returning from Bird Heaven.

We drive to Bird Heaven and it's sad. The water is gone and there are large dried-up cracks in the ground with small grass-like plants growing between them. The energetic temple on the platform feels old and abandoned. There are only a few birds. I do a soil balancing for all of the wildlife refuge, then a soil balancing for the area underneath the platform. Then I do an energy clearing for all of the refuge and an energy clearing for the platform and temple. As a result, the temple is becoming reactivated.

Then, I ask Sky to play. I connect all the Mimzy points and ask that this linkage reactivate this temple. After Sky plays for a bit, I feel a distracting energy from a rear corner of the platform. There's a bench there and I move to sit on it and the energy goes away. Sky's bowl playing reawakens the temple even further. After a moment, I feel this temple connect to the one at the headwaters of the Sacramento River and I feel and almost hear the connection snap into place.

After she plays, I leave a crystal beneath the platform to stabilize the positive energy and one under the entry walkway. I ask the crystals to continue to remind the temple that it is a temple.

We drive to Klamath Falls, entering the town via Business Highway 97. We purposely drive around the depressed area of the center city, sending love and light as we go. Finally we reach the motel, but find that it is full. We call a few other motels in our price range, but they are all also full. A motel in Weed, 71 miles away, has plenty of empty rooms, so we retrace our route back almost to Bird Heaven, then all the way to Weed. We stop at Rumbling Point to eat our half sandwiches that we never finished at lunch. We arrive at Weed around 8 p.m., tired from our dramatic day.

Autumn Equinox at Stewart Mineral Springs

The next day, we arrive at Stewart Mineral Springs about 2 p.m. and begin taking wonderful cleansing baths. Zara arrives as prearranged and begins her bath. While soaking, I connect the mineral springs with all the Mimzy points. When I'm finished bathing, I use hot water from an electric kettle to sterilize a dropper bottle. Then I use brandy and five drops of the mother essence to make a bottle of slender penstemon essence for Zara.

After the baths, we go to the gazebo near the place where the white spring water (masculine) and the red spring water (feminine) flow together. I place a crystal that wants to be part of this ceremony on the altar. Sky asks Zara to read from *The Seventy-two Sacred Names of the Myriad Expressions of the Living God.* Luckily, Zara has brought the book. Her guides had sent her back to get it as she was leaving her house. Zara chants or sings each name and we chant or sing with her as best we can. After each name, Sky hits her bowl like a gong. It takes a long time to do the whole ceremony. Afterward, my crystal wants to be left in the stream, so I toss it there.

We go to our room and eat humus, crackers, pears, and grapes. Zara and Sky drink green tea. We talk about our lives and Zara tells us a bit of her history. A few minutes before the equinox moment, we gather in a circle and hold hands. I say a few words about how the autumn equinox is the time in nature that the call goes out to start the next cycle. And that we can call in the start of the next cycle in our own personal evolution as well.

We have a few moments of silence while the equinox moment passes. Zara hugs us both and leaves. I wonder when I'll see her again.

CIRCLING BACK

We complete the last segment of our circuitous journey by returning home. Driving through Chico, we somehow get off the main route and end up circling around another depressed area, sending out light and love in our now-familiar way.

That evening, we see our fellow Mimzy collaborators, Ursa, Tricia, and Sybil. We also have a day of rest and reorganization before Sky and Ursa leave for further adventures.

I miss Sky almost as soon as she leaves, but I know I'll see her again and we'll continue our enlightening and enlivening adventures.

CHAPTER 6

ESSENCES OF FLOWERS

In the fall of 2010, I rejoined the writing class and wrote the following during one of our class sessions.

THE BEGINNING OF JOY

We ride with the Sun into our future. If "future" be what you name it. We ride with the Sun into a section of space where the ever-spiraling waves of energy are more intense. The increasing intensity of these waves is causing the changes we are now experiencing. As inevitable a change as night changing into day.

Each of us requested the opportunity to be here for the "show," and each of us was one of the ones chosen. Thank goodness if your remembrance of this is solid and can be relied on. It abides within as other things pass away.

What of those who can't remember or don't want to remember, those who are hankering for a less intense time and refuse to be pulled kicking and screaming into the future of our planet? They just say no. Thank goodness for them that they don't have to go. The wonderful rules of soul development say that they can take all the time they please. Or the rules would say that if "time" was real. Instead of "time," we could more properly call the changes our souls are going through "lushness." They can use all the lovely lushness they need. They can extravagantly drape themselves in gossamer silks of lushness and wear sparkling lush jewels and eat banquets of lush foods, until they're as stuffed and sated with it as they want to be. There's no worry, no hurry.

Beyond this small realization, there is a greater one: There is a unity of souls. Our souls are created as droplets spun out from the ocean of the Great Creator. Each soul is infinitely beautiful and precious. This is reality. We are no better, no worse, no higher, no lower than any other soul. All of us are mutually creating our universe and our world from our soul consciousness.

Can you take your stand in that field of reality and hold firm? Refuse to budge from it no matter what your veiled mind may tell you? Each soul is infinitely beautiful and precious. Can you see each person you meet as that? Can you see yourself as that? Can you smile at each person from your soul, pushing aside the veil for a moment, so you both can see the transcendent reality behind it? In this is the end of self-judgment and the beginning of joy.

A PECULIAR SORROW

As we moved toward the holiday season in December 2010, I experienced a particular sadness. Like most mothers, I have always been able to sense the presence of my children in the world, even though they are now grown and I do not always know where they are. But during this time, I was not able to sense the presence of my younger son, Thor—not because of any particular trouble or complaint between us. It was as if his heart was closed to me, and darkness existed between us. In my struggles to gain equanimity about this, I wrote the following passage in my journal.

I Can't Find Him: Journal Entry, December 8, 2010

I can't find him in my dreaming. Last night I looked, and I may have glimpsed him. He was there like a shadow behind his brother, Dickon. Only because I saw Dickon did I realize that the other one there—the shadow—was probably Thor. Right now Dickon is the one who links us; we can only see each other darkly through him.

I'm not sure why this matters or why the current separation brings me sadness. I'm sure that there will be a time in the future when we are together in light. So that is sufficient. It's not necessary to untangle the current situation or to understand why this separation is present. It's just story anyway and doesn't have any more relevance than the news does to what is really happening in the world. Worry and sadness and longing are ineffective uses of my resources, and I know this, so I will vigilantly detach myself from them and turn my attention to more productive and happier thoughts. I will clear out my chakras, bring in light, and go on with my day, working with others who ask for connection, and putting aside in my mind the one I love who does not ask.

You know, I've done this before. Almost everyone has. There's the end of a love affair when the other wants to leave before you are ready. It's not your choice, but you must accept, know it's over, and move on. There's suffering, you try to move it out of your field and focus on other things, knowing that it will get better and your life will fill up with love again. With the love affair, you can cut your ties to the other completely or you can just loosen them and put lots of space between both of you for a year or two. Then sometimes, if you're lucky and the other person also wants it, you can find each other again in a lifelong friendship. This is what happened between me and my close friend whom I know, love, and trust down to the ground of my being, as he does me.

With your child, the option of cutting ties completely doesn't exist. Or at least it doesn't exist as an option for me, and I don't believe it exists for my son either. So there is another resolution in store for us. Maybe I'll try the plan that worked so well for my friend and me those decades ago: put lots of space and light between us for a year or two, and see what happens.

AN ACCIDENT AND A REVERSAL

Within a few days after writing the previous entry in my journal, the situation dramatically changed. Thor and Dickon's stepmother was killed in a tragic accident. Thor was shaken to his core, and his heart burst open. At the memorial, he told me, "Mom, someone can drive you crazy, but you should enjoy them while you can, because you never know how long you will have with them." Since that moment, I have been able to feel Thor's presence in the world, even if I don't know where he is or what he's doing.

LUNAR ECLIPSE, WINTER SOLSTICE 2010

Lunar eclipse. Magic in the moonlight. The solstice drawing us closer to that which is coming. I feel it drawing me like a tide. I want to be swept away in its beguiling waters and flung out on the shore of destiny, my hair in tangles and my heart bewitched by the pulse of the universe flowing through me.

And so it will be.

BLUE SAPPHIRE

I bought two blue sapphire stones. I put them alongside the petrified bamboo that lives in the ceramic incense holder that forms a small altar beside my bed. Not in my office with most of the other stones and crystals, but beside my bed with the flower essence crystal; the small, green, translucent moldavite; the spirit crystal; and the Mimzy crystal, which is almost lavender.

Why did I buy the two blue sapphires? Because in a light-filled time and space, Zara called in both her guides and my guides, and relayed to me some things I would need. One was a gold essence. I created the essence using flecks of gold that Skidmore collected with his gold pan during lazy summer days spent at the river in California's Gold County. I started taking a few drops of the gold essence every day. Another was to wear more gold, so I started wearing the necklace Skidmore gave me when we first loved each other, before we knew each other down to the ground.

Lastly, the guides told me I would need a blue sapphire essence later on. Now that I have the stones, I can make the essence whenever I find that the right time has come.

I love absolutely every glorious drop of all this. I feel as though I could run on all day telling you all the details and every last morsel of all the absolutely fabulous things that are happening each and every day. Six impossible things before breakfast. I think tomorrow I'll make it seven.

What did I do to deserve all this? I know I've worked long and hard and diligently, but even so, I can't deserve it. It must be grace, pure and simple. Grace is flowing everywhere, and I've just accepted it, welcomed it home, and made it my own.

Why blue sapphire essence? What will the blue sapphire energy balance?

When I was 14, our family visited the New York World's Fair. There are only two things I remember distinctly from our visit. The first memorable thing was the look, taste, and crunchy feel of Belgian waffles. Today you can order these at IHOP, and they are not the special and unique food that they were in 1964 when you had to go all the way to New York, if not to Belgium, to get them. They were layered three waffles deep and covered with strawberries and whipped cream, and I thought they were the food of the gods.

My other distinct memory from the World's Fair is the glory of the sunlight passing through blue stained glass that was focused on Michelangelo's Pietà, the most beautiful, graceful, and sorrowful statue I have ever seen. The blue light, the sorrow, and the transcendence of that moment are somehow connected with the blue sapphire essence. When I see that pattern of blueness in my life again, I will create and then take the blue sapphire essence.

UNIQUELY SHAPED: JOURNAL ENTRY, JANUARY 26, 2011

Vibrant green. A local farmer says he's never seen a cover crop so vibrantly green as the crop in my front yard's raised beds. Daffodils spring up alongside our driveway. The chickens are brooding. It's as if we're having spring in January. People are more vibrant as well. There's an extra sparkle in my husband's eyes. Each person's unique shape is clearer and more precious. Sometimes I think I can hardly stand so much beauty.

I remember the 1950s and how black and white the world seemed then. As in the movie *The Wizard of Oz*, the black and white of the '50s changed into the Kodachrome of the late '60s. I remember the excitement and newly found freedom of those days when we pushed boundaries and explored the realm of self, bringing in many new ideas in such a short amount of time.

Despite the pushback of Reaganomics, the corporate world reasserting its control over our economy and government, and the world's seemingly endless warfare, we have been doing the hard work of grounding the principles of equality and justice into our laws, our workplaces, and our most intimate relationships. This work is ongoing and has made a decisive impact on the American nation.

Look at the diversity of the leaders the United States has today—all races and both sexes are represented. During his first term, President Obama even appointed a transgender person to work at the White House. On a video she posted on YouTube, her message to us was to be your unique self, and if at first you are not accepted, stay true to yourself and things will get better. In time, you will find yourself among those who believe in you and you will make a difference in the world.

The past 40 years has been a hard slog of working to bring the possibilities unveiled in the late '60s to fruition today.

Recently, the times have again shifted. Now we awaken each day to excitement and immense possibility. Our current era is a time of such an intense inflowing of energy that it makes the '60s look staid by comparison. The '60s were like a "dress rehearsal." This decade is the "performance" itself. Everyone is caught up in the increasing waves of energy that are engulfing our planet. People who are successfully riding the energy waves are flowing, their soul shapes are more perceptible to all.

Other people are not riding the energy waves. They are trying to stop the energy, stop the changes. They are living in profound fear and struggle. Instead of seeing vibrant colors, they see darkness and the blood red of anger. They are missing the beauty, the joy, and the excitement. They are missing the opportunity to refine the shape of who they are in their unique souls. To change or remain unchanged is a choice they are free to make, as universal law gives free will to all souls. I salute them all and wish them well on their journey.

My wish for each person who hears or reads my words is that you enjoy every drop of the sweet heady nectar of these glorious times.

FROM THE PWN HANDBOOK

Before the planting season begins each spring, I connect with Nature and ask, "Of all the fertilizers stocked by our local organic supply store, which should I buy?"

In 2011, I was guided to buy seven new fertilizers: a local-mix fertilizer formulated for the local region, Greensand, Kelp Meal, a liquid fertilizer with zinc, a 4-10-7 fertilizer, Bone Meal, and a tomato and vegetable fertilizer 5-7-3.

Okay, I thought, *so far so good.*

As Skidmore and I were preparing our vegetable beds and clearing out water wells for our trees, I started to get an idea of where these fertilizers were to be used. The local-mix fertilizer was going into all the vegetable beds. I found this out by asking Nature bed by bed. The tomato and vegetable fertilizer, not surprisingly, was going into the two tomato beds. The squash and bean beds were getting the same, plus Greensand.

If you're wondering how I know which vegetables to

plant and which beds to put them in, the answer is easy: I ask Nature. That is, I ask Nature after telling Nature how many people I want to feed and how much produce I want to put up to eat later. It's our job to specify for Nature the purpose and desired outcomes of any project, whether it's a garden, a business, or another enterprise.

This year, when I asked about fertilizer for our trees and grapes, I got some unexpected answers. When you work this way yourself, expect unexpected answers. For example, our male pineapple guava trees needed Kelp Meal, but our female pineapple guava trees didn't need any fertilizer. One of our pear trees, a sickly looking one, needed Kelp Meal and the 4-10-7 fertilizer, while the other pear tree needed nothing. Our young grapes also needed the 4-10-7 fertilizer, while our established grapes needed nothing.

I could go on through the whole list, but you get the idea. There's no way I could have figured this out by myself. It's a great relief to have someone to ask who knows the answers.

Thanks, Nature!

A SERENDIPITOUS BOOK: JOURNAL ENTRY, MARCH 15, 2011, SHAMANIC VALLEY CAMPGROUND

The strident sounds of military planes rent the air as I prepare to write in my journal. It's might trying to make right. The tangible reality of these hot springs will remain when war has passed away.

Two days ago I was stung by a wasp, a sting that has not completely yielded to homeopathic remedies. Of these, *Apis* has helped the most, yet I felt ill most of yesterday, and today the area around the sting is still swollen and inflamed. Yesterday I also began to read *The Shamanic Way of the Bee* by

Simon Buxton. Is it a coincidence that I should begin this book under the influence of a sting? I no longer believe in that kind of coincidence. My life is too blessed with the magic of serendipity.

The book and the sting are clearly an initiation preceding some sort of shift or change—I know not what, except that it seems probably connected to the beehives that I intend to ask some local beekeepers to bring onto our land. These hives are in turn connected to the flower essence plants I will be planting upon my return.

CHANGE AND CHANGELESSNESS: JOURNAL ENTRY, MARCH 16, 2011, SHAMANIC VALLEY CAMPGROUND

Spaceship clouds every day but one. Dreams of the Clintons. Secretary Gates stands like a sentinel. Nuclear reactor meltdown in Japan. Things are moving fast, changing our planet, even as I sit in the changelessness of nature's sanctuary here in Shamanic Valley.

A SUPERNAL EXPERIENCE: JOURNAL ENTRY, MAY 4, 2011

It's 1956 and my sister and I are riding in the back seat of my parent's blue Oldsmobile, the blue car that my father called *green* because he was color blind. My parents in the front, seen through my six-year-old eyes, look old. Looking back today, seeing them in the rearview mirror of my mind, they look so young, so new and hopeful. We are driving up the road to Sandia Peak, looking for a nice picnic spot to spend a lovely summer Sunday.

Three years before, we had moved from our home in the Midwest to a Southwestern town, ostensibly for my mother's arthritis, the fore sign of the dementia that would one day encase her. In reality, we moved to escape the overbearing "familiness" of my mother's large Irish-Catholic family. As my father later told me, my parents didn't want to spend every Sunday morning in church and every Sunday afternoon with relatives.

This Sunday, my parents have brought blankets and the newspaper so they can lie down and read it in a beautiful spot on their one day of rest and relaxation before taking up the challenges of their working day lives again. My mother, unlike the other moms on our block, owns her own business and goes to work every day except Sunday.

After considering and discarding several likely sites, we find the perfect spot we are looking for, a place we can pull off the road, away from the view of passing cars, with a level area for our picnic. As my parents are spreading their blankets and unloading the cooler, my sister and I jump out of the car and run up the side of the mountain. We are running up through the steep pine forest for the sheer joy of stretching our legs and exploring whatever we may find.

In our different windings through the trees, we soon become separated. I'm enjoying the delicious feeling of being alone after the enclosed car ride. I continue climbing the mountain, enjoying how the view below becomes more panoramic the higher I climb. Finally, I stop and select a sunny spot to sit. Pine trees surround me. Birds twitter, and insects hum and buzz around me. Opposite slopes across the small valley are also covered with pine trees. Pine scent infuses the fresh oxygenated air.

As I sit drinking in the loveliness, something unusual begins to happen. My legs seem to disappear in a strange way, as if they are somehow fusing into the ground. A mysterious agent lifts my spirit up and out of my normal boundaries and I begin perceiving from a higher, expanded location. It's so beautiful! All is infused with an ineffable light. I've never experienced this before, yet it is anciently familiar. My heart is awash in an infinite love . . . the love in which I move and have my being. By some unknown dispensation, I've been granted the joy of experiencing the ground of all being here on this mountain.

My six-year-old mind doesn't know how to frame this experience except to envision that Christ is here on the mountain, speaking to me through the beauty of nature. My heart speaks back, saying repeatedly, "I love you. I love you."

I sit transfixed for some time, and then the supernal sensations gradually fade away. I slowly get up and carefully begin the walk back to my family below me. Instead of my normal careless way of walking, in which I'm really thinking about other matters, I find I now must concentrate my mind on my motions. Control of my physical body is not assured. When I reach my family, they remark that I was gone for quite a while. I brush this aside, not wanting to speak about the indescribable. No one in my family ever had such an experience—at least they have never spoken of one. How can I speak of something so intimate with those who can never understand?

I date my connection to mountains to this, my first experience of transcendence. From the patio of my childhood home, I could see Sandia Peak. In the years ahead, as I grew up, I would often sit there and connect with the mountain in the distance. Its silent steadiness comforted me, a lonely, bookish girl who felt like a stranger in a strange land.

From the PWN Handbook

Soil can be balanced energetically using a tiny amount of minerals and flower essences. It's easy to do. First, you define the boundaries of the area you wish to work with. Then you connect to the Deva of Soil, Pan, and the rest of your partnership team, and ask, "What minerals are needed to balance the soil?"

You should have small vials of bone meal, kelp, and other natural fertilizers with you when you ask, so that and you can use kinesiology to test which ones are needed. When you get your answer, put a tiny amount of each needed fertilizer in a spoon and ask Pan to transfer it energetically into the soil. Wait a minute for the transfer to take place.

Afterwards, you can stabilize the balancing of the soil with flower essences. Using kinesiology, test which essences are needed. Put a few drops of each needed essence in a spoon, and again ask Pan to energetically transfer them for the stabilization of your process.

Soil balancing does not eliminate the need for fertilizers, as it energetically strengthens the soil without changing its material composition. However, we can change the soil, and thereby change the plants and food we grow, much more easily in this way than by using conventional fertilizer and compost alone.

Raising Chicks

I love having chickens, and raising them the natural way. I want chicks to have the experience of hatching out from under a mother and being raised by her care, according to the natural design for their species.

In 2011, the weather got warm in March and fooled our

plum tree into blossoming, only to lose its setting fruit during subsequent freezes. One of our chickens got broody at the same time, but abandoned the nest when the weather turned cold again.

I was just starting to think about buying baby chicks when the same hen finally started setting in earnest again. We call this particular hen Rocky because she's a barred Plymouth Rock bantam. She hatched and raised ten babies the year before, and she was a great mother. We moved her to a quiet nesting space to sit for 21 days until the birth of the chicks. I admire her quiet devotion to the duties of chick rearing and aspire to complete my own tasks in such a finished way.

FUKUSHIMA FEARS

In spring 2011, many people on the West Coast were experiencing fear of being impacted by radiation from the Fukushima reactor disaster in Japan. Clients were asking me what they could do to protect themselves. I heard so much of this type of discussion that I started to react against the fear that inspired it.

In writing class, my teacher, Denna, quoted from John O'Donohue, "And waste my heart on fear no more." The quote affected me powerfully. A doorway inside me burst open and the following passionate declaration poured out.

MANIFESTO

I'm not afraid of the water. I'm not afraid of the air. I'm not afraid to eat the vegetables I will grow this summer. I'm not afraid of the Sun. I'm not afraid of economic collapse. I'm not afraid of government shutdowns. I will waste my heart on fear no more.

You who have eyes to see, see how the water is more sparkling and fresh than ever. I want to jump into the water from a high rock above and plunge into its depth, my hair streaming behind me. And then, once the inertia of the plunge is spent, release all effort and allow the buoyancy of my body to bring me to the surface where I shall fill my lungs with fresh pure air, supplying joy and sustenance through my blood stream to all my cells.

This is the right of all who live on this planet. Clean clear water, fresh pure air, and empowering Sun. And so it is and so it will be as we claim it as our birthright, put aside fear, and accept no substitutes. No trading off for job security. No trading off for material so-called wealth, which is really the impoverishment of a chained life. No trading off for the so-called welfare of all, as in, "We can't grow enough organic food to feed everyone."

We refuse to trade off pure nourishment for any so-called reason that can be given. This is where we take our stand and demand clean, pure, light-filled water and air, sunlight, and food for ourselves and our planet.

This manifesto is not a call for political action, although it will result in action that will bring change to our governments. It's not a call for economic action, although our economies will be changed. It's a call for each person to stand firmly grounded on Earth and declare that our planet will henceforth operate as it was designed. For each person to declare that he or she will accept no substitute designs or plans, regardless of what beguiling enticements may be offered, enticements that appear to offer safety, but really only offer a walled off life shielded from the full experience of being human on this planet.

Then, as we take our stand, here we are. Ours is a changed life, a changed government, a changed economy. Our precious Earth is vibrant with life, with rolling green hills, sparkling water, and fresh air, with vegetables and fruits full of vitamins, minerals, and flavor. We stand in our bare feet with our toes buried in the soil, and give thanks for such bounty and the magnificence of our life here on this loveliest of planets.

FROM THE PWN HANDBOOK

One of the ongoing projects that I'm working on with Nature involves the making of flower essences, and the creation of a flower essence company called Celestial Gardens. The project involves growing flowers, and then creating and bottling flower essences from them. The unique energetic pattern of each flower is to be transferred into an essence.

To create the flower essences, I have some supplies, such as raised beds, fertilizer, and gardening tools. I also have information on each flower to be grown: its botanical name, what kind of sun or shade it likes, whether it's an annual or perennial, and when to plant it. So far, so good.

On the energetic level, I have supplies of another kind: land that the Nature spirits love, where they can live and express themselves in freedom, and my genesa crystal, which pulls in energy from within a mile radius, cleans it, and spins it back out. It's a continuous energy filtration device. Most importantly, I have my team of Nature spirits and other guides. They are constantly available to me, helping me with every detail. They let me know which seed to plant, where, and when. What fertilizer each plant needs. How much and when to water. The crucial moment to pick the blossoms. The exact procedure needed to transmute the essence from the petals of the flower into water. Then finally, the exact procedure to bond the essence more strongly to the water, and preserve it in brandy for purity over time.

When working on my flower essence project, every decision Nature and I make together must be recorded. The procedures we have developed together are unique and do not exactly conform to those that were previously in use by other essence manufacturers. We are helping create a new map of what flower essences are, and of how they are to be used. In time, we will also be including the flowers of new plants in our compendium of essences. These new plants will be able to grow on our planet once the necessary conditions are present to support them.

The archetypes of such flowers already exist, and they may actually be already growing on other planets that are experiencing a higher dimension of consciousness than our own. Once our planet shifts to a higher frequency, these archetypes may find that they can actualize here, at which point I can work with them.

This is actually the way that evolution happens, not through random changes in the DNA of existing plants, as is commonly thought. Instead, these seemingly random changes in DNA are a deliberate change, initiated by an archetype in order to manifest a new plant. Everything in physical form must have had an existence in consciousness first, or it would not be here. Remember, the archetype or deva is the blueprint in consciousness for that particular form. The Nature spirit for that form works with the archetype to ground that form into physical reality on our planet.

In the case of plants, the seeds carry the DNA and are the transmission device for the germination of new plants. But the seeds alone cannot create new life. New life can form and grow only through the action of an archetype and the Nature spirits.

This is why genetically modified (GMO) crops are barely alive, and do not carry enough life force to feed our bodies. We are trying to supplant Nature's archetype with one of our own. The Nature spirit for GMO plants can't properly align with the true archetype of those plants. So the amount of vital force that can be held by the plant is extremely limited.

This is the opposite of what is occurring on my land, where the garden is radiant with vital force. The flowers I grow are infused with this vital energy, allowing the creation of potent flower essences.

NURTURING THE FLOWER, RECEIVING THE PATTERN

Flower essences. Each gifts us with a unique healing pattern. I am taking plants that I've raised from seed, moving them from my greenhouse, and anchoring them into nutrient-rich, fertile soil. I have three raised beds ready to receive them.

Before I plant, I ask each plant to tell me which bed it wants to settle in. Once I know the bed, I can sense where in the bed it wants to be. With the plant container in my right hand, I sense an attraction between the plant and a spot in the bed. It feels like one magnet subtly being drawn toward another. I place the container in that spot, and then continue arranging the other plants destined for the same bed until the bed is dotted with plants in their containers.

Once I've found a place for each container, I ask the plants if everyone is happy. Usually most are, but one or two are not. I switch the different plant containers around until each plant is content and feels supported by its immediate neighbors. Then I plant.

As I plant, I can feel each plant release its rootedness energy into the soil. It is such a blessed relief for the plants to move from the artificial environment of crowded containers on a greenhouse shelf to the more expansive and less artificial environment of soil in a raised bed. They can finally allow themselves to sink down and engage in the business of expanding their roots, growing leaves and stalks, and receiving water and nutrients. The factory that is a plant has plenty to do.

Each day I watch over them. Do they have enough water? Do they need more fertilizer or compost tea? Are insects disturbing them more than the normal give and take that belongs in the garden? If there is some imbalance, perhaps I can assist them with a homeopathic remedy.

The plants are aware of my thoughts, my caring. There is an understanding between us, a compact that includes the reason we are doing all of this. At the right time, at the height of their powers, I will ask them to fully transfer the healing pattern they hold into the flower, so that I may harvest the petals. Then I will ask the petals to release the healing pattern fully into sunlit water. I will take the resulting elixir, preserve it with brandy, and stabilize it with tensor energy and a crystal. This becomes the "mother essence" from which I can create additional small bottles of Celestial Gardens Balance Drops. At the end of the whole process, a healing pattern has been transferred into water and bottled into medicine.

Each essence is a gift from Nature to us, designed especially for the healing of the human body and mind. I'm filled with gratitude for these gifts and for the gift of being allowed to be a part of the celestial grounding process.

When I made my first flower essence in Panther Meadows in the fall of 2010, I used whatever supplies I happened to have with me. I had no precise instructions from Nature to work with, so I just used my knowledge of how flower essences are made in general.

Since then I have worked with my Nature team to develop the precise steps to be used for all the essences we will be making together. In June 2011, I created my second flower essence from a butterfly bush plant (*Buddleja Davidii*). The plant is one Zara had visualized me growing, and I found it at a local nursery. I planned to plant it in our small orchard, but on planting day, it wanted to be planted in a flower bed that Zara had cleared out below the window of our guest room. The plant had violet masses of tiny flowers growing in a conical shape. I took over 20 of the best of these tiny flowers to make its mother essence.

Later that summer, I created five essences from flowers that I had grown from seed: white bishop's lace (*Ammi majus*), *Calendula officinalis*, *Delphinium* (Larkspur), hedge mustard (*Sisymbrium officinale*), and lupine (*Lupinus polyphyllus*). I also made essences from two plants that were growing wild in my area: elegant brodiaea (*Brodiaea elegans*) and St. John's wort (*Hypericum perforatum*).

I had forgotten that I had planted belladonna lily (A*maryllis belladonna*) bulbs in my flower bed, so I was surprised when I found them growing there. They were breathtakingly beautiful, so I was gratified that my team wanted them made into an essence, too.

THE LAST QUARTER INCH:
JOURNAL ENTRY, AUGUST 17, 2011

The last quarter inch. We have to do it—all of us, not just those who are spiritually awake. Each of us has to stop playing the character we've been playing and find the self within that blesses all. That's the only way through the eye of the needle, and we have to do it as one global people.

We are being wedged. We want the world's governments to do it, but they are gridlocked. We want our financial systems and banks to do it, but they are bankrupt. We look everywhere outside for salvation, but wherever we look, the way is blocked. We are kicking and screaming, and behaving badly as we are forced back onto the ground of our being, our stories broken into dusty fragments and scattered to the winds. From this ground of being, we look with new eyes and have the grace to see others as they are, and to offer sustenance to those in need.

I've thought a lot about new structures for a new age—new forms of economy, new agriculture, new medicine. I've imagined how sustainable structures could be built and function. We will need much creativity and cooperation to put new structures like these in place. Yet all of the outer work of manifesting new forms is the easy part and will flow naturally and with unprecedented speed once the real transformative action has taken place within us as individuals.

Fortunately, a person doesn't need to consciously understand anything about the nature of change and why changes are happening in our social structures. We are all being wedged through the chute and each person must decide what to abandon: the inner truth in the ground of their being, or their stories.

In the past, individual people or groups of people have been forced to make this decision. Now it's all of us. Higher vibrations surrounding our planet are now supporting us in making a soul-born choice. We will all jump the last quarter inch together.

A Fire Clearing Proposal

One project with Nature that opened up in a way beyond Skidmore and my imagining was the fire-clearing project. We had already cleared a 30-foot circle of defensible space around our house in accordance with good fire-prevention techniques. When clearing an area in this way, you don't have to remove every tree. You can just clear out the brush and remove the lower branches of trees.

The rest of the undeveloped part of the land, maybe about five acres, we left undisturbed, as the domain of Nature and a habitat for animals. I seldom walk there, and then only as a visitor to Nature's special preserve where Nature spirits can live freely without human involvement in their affairs.

Almost every visitor to our home is aware of the restful, healing ambiance that surrounds the place. People comment that it feels good just to be there. Those that are sensitive to Nature spirits immediately feel their pervading presence as soon as they arrive and open their car doors.

Since I considered the undeveloped area to be sacrosanct to Nature, I was concerned when we began to discuss further clearing. I cherished the uplifting feeling of having multitudes of Nature spirits so nearby. If we began tramping around their area and taking out trees and brush, would they leave the property? I really wanted them to have the security of knowing that there was one area on this hill where they wouldn't be disturbed.

In late August 2011, Skidmore requested an evaluation from a brush-clearing company to specify how trees and brush on our land could best be removed to make our house safer in case of fire. Their proposal was to clear 100 to 150 feet of land around the house, all the way down the hill to our firebreak road. All the trees and brush in the entire area would be removed. More than an acre of wildlife habitat would be destroyed in order to make our home safer in case of a fire that might never come. The plan was so drastic and the justifications given for it were so unreasonable to me, that I wrote the following passionate response to the recommendations in my journal.

AN EDIFICE OF CRAZY THINKING

A 100- to 150-foot fire clearing has been suggested for our home. It's brutal. No suggestion of the possibility of working with Nature to determine what should be removed and what can stay. Destruction of plant and animal habitat proposed to be done in case of fire, something that may not ever happen. The clearing man says that the insurance companies are now requiring this; and that if I were the owner of the insurance company I'd also be insisting that it be done—as if owners of insurance companies can't also be good citizens of the Earth. Apparently, money trumps everything, even the survival of humankind on this planet. And here's the kicker: The cleared space will soon fill up with growth again, but most likely with invasive species. So in order to protect our investment in clearing, we'll need to use herbicides; otherwise, we'll just be wasting money.

This recommendation is wrong in so many ways that my mind gridlocks just thinking about it. First, there's the assumption that fire is a bad thing and might come even if it's not in the highest interest of all. Second is the assumption that Nature has no investment in this land and will do nothing to protect it, and will wantonly destroy it if left uncontrolled.

Third is the assumption that I can't work with Nature to

determine what would best be removed and how to remove it.

Fourth is the assumption that it's a bad thing that Nature will fill the cleared area up again with life.

Fifth is the assumption that when Nature attempts to fill it up again with life, we need to use poison to control and thwart Nature. By the way, they say this poison is okay because it only needs to be used for a few hours once a year.

The sixth assumption is that the act of poisoning life won't energetically affect all the other life that is on the land.

The seventh assumption is that poisoning life in the cleared area won't also affect the organic vegetables and flower essences that are growing a relatively short distance away. Not to mention the bees, butterflies, and hummingbirds that we depend on for pollination and the birds we depend on to eat insects in the gardens.

The eighth and final assumption is that we wouldn't actually want to hire real people who needed work to maintain the cleared space, because, you see, that would cost more money.

All this crazy edifice of layered thinking is driven by fire departments and insurance companies, and even more particularly by the fear of fire. And the most discouraging part to me is that my husband, in his fear of fire, buys into this thinking. You'd never know that we actually pay a fair amount of money for fire insurance so that we can be more relaxed about the possibility of fire. This is a possibility that always exists wherever you live, but especially here in our partially forested countryside.

Please know that my lack of extreme fear around fire doesn't mean that I think a certain amount of prudent clearing shouldn't be done. When we first got the place, I worked with Nature to determine a protocol for dealing with the poison oak that would work for us and for Nature. For clearing, I can easily work with Nature again to determine which trees and bushes should be removed, which should be trimmed, and which should remain untouched. The task is fairly straightforward. It's the thinking around me that is my special challenge.

Hopefully I will find a way to bring sanity to this situation—and who knows, it just might educate or inspire someone around me.

THE FIRE CLEARING PROJECT

Skidmore was still uneasy. I talked to Nature about it, and found willingness for some type of clearing to be done. So one day, Skidmore and I walked out into this area, the part of our land I call the *realm of the wild and the sweet.* My intention was to ask individually about each bush or tree. Was it to be left as is, trimmed up from the bottom, or removed entirely?

I soon find that I don't need to identify each tree or bush individually. Nature wants all the buckbrush removed, all the toyon to remain as is, and all the lower manzanita branches to be trimmed. Nature wants this done down to the firebreak road and the remaining area below the road to be left as tangled wildness. Nature also wants any trees or bushes that are starting to impinge on the firebreak road to be trimmed back.

Skidmore begins acting on this plan, removing or clearing as directed. What begins to happen amazes me, and reinforces again that when working with Nature I should expect the unexpected.

I have been regarding the clearing as a necessary evil and certainly not as something that would actually be welcomed by

Nature. But as Skidmore begins clearing away the buckbrush and burning it, I feel a palpable sense of relief from Nature. The Nature spirits actually want the buckbrush gone! Clearly there is more of it than is ideal for whatever plans Nature has in mind.

I am also amazed by another unexpected change. With the buckbrush removed and the manzanita trimmed up, the rock outcroppings are uncovered and their loveliness revealed. The presence of the rock spirits becomes more evident and their contribution to the uplifting feel of the land becomes apparent.

About the same time, we begin to attend monthly meetings of the local beekeepers club in order to prepare ourselves to acquire and care for two beehives. I had been aware for some time that Nature wanted the presence of bees on the land. The previous year I had tried to persuade local beekeepers to keep some hives at our place without success. So we decide that this year we will learn to tend bees ourselves.

One of the decisions we need to make is where to best locate the hives. A sunny area near a road, but not too near the house, with a southern or western orientation would be ideal. It turns out that during our fire clearing project we had cleared an area where the hives could be located with plenty of sun and a southwestern orientation just off our firebreak road. Perfect!

While looking at this proposed hive area, it suddenly dawns on me that the entire cleared-out area can be more easily navigated by the bees. They can easily whizz around among the toyon and manzanita now that the other brush is gone. And when not in a whizzing mood, they can fly more carefully into the untamed area across the firebreak road. I begin to suspect that this is what Nature had in mind all along: bees, a more park-like area for them to fly around in, and a stronger influence for the rock spirits. What I had been thinking of as two projects, the clearing and the beekeeping, are probably one project to Nature.

I'm delighted anew with the fun, synchronicity, and adventure of being a student of Nature's curriculum.

THISTLE ESSENCES

In September 2011, I harvest bull thistle (*Cirsium vulgare*) at Denna's Apple Valley Farm. I'm happy to have thistles that grew within her vibration. I immediately transport them in a wet cloth, arriving home around 20 minutes later.

I take photos of the plants I've gathered, and then start to make the essence. I just use the top, purple part of the head, cutting it off from the white part below. Soon I have a great many very thin short purple "dashes" floating on the water. When the essence is done, it takes about half an hour more to remove them all with a skimmer and a strainer before bottling the mother essence in the jars I've set aside for this purpose.

The next day, I gather yellow star thistle plants (*Centaurea solstitialis*) from behind our garage. I remove the spines, and then cut off the top yellow part of each flower, which mostly holds together in a loose clump—one clump from each flower. It's amazing to see how cheerful and tender the flowers look floating in the water, detached from their spines and bristly branches.

When subsequently bottling this essence, images of rape and murder come into my mind. This is a plant that is much despised in my area, the target of continuous attempts to eradicate and poison it. I'm aware that it will probably be a healing essence for those who have been abused.

MAKING A FLOWER ESSENCE

Sun, a glass bowl, petals from a freshly picked blossom, pure water. I am using these seemingly simple ingredients to create an etheric elixir, a flower essence. My desire, my need, my longing to create this subtle substance was born in ancient days and nurtured in lifetimes of service to the calling of energetic healing.

Today, I invoke again my partnership with Nature spirits and with the collective that stands in solidarity for the cause of human evolution on our planet, which is commonly called *the Great White Brotherhood*. The glass bowl of energized water and floating petals sits upon a woven cloth on a stand in the sun. I cup my hands below the curve of the bowl, one on each side, almost touching the glass. I stand in anticipation, readying myself in silence, preparing to link words and action into a single request. The moment arrives, I draw light from above down through my crown chakra into my heart, and out through my hands while humbly, but surely, requesting that the petals release their healing pattern into the water. I stand in this stream of light for a few moments, then thank my colleagues and partners, and move away. The bowl will remain in the sun for a few more hours while the petals complete their task of release.

Later I return and carry the bowl into my house, where I bottle it into four one-quart mason jars and preserve it with French brandy. Then I stabilize each quart with my genesa crystal and a particular arrangement of other stones and crystals that I've been given to use.

I again stand in silence, a quart of essence placed within the genesa crystal before me. Again I ready myself and cup my hands around the jar. I draw in light through my crown, through my heart, and send it out my hands. I ask that the energies of this essence, the energies of this genesa, and the energies of these stones and crystals be fused into one stable healing pattern.

I stand for a moment transfixed in this field of light and subtle energies and give thanks for the grace of being able to perform this sacred work of heaven and earth.

PENSTEMON GRACILENTUS (SLENDER PENSTEMON)

Later in September, I return to Panther Meadows to make the slender penstemon essence according to my new instructions. I camp at the same site where I had made a smaller amount of the essence of the same flower exactly a year earlier. This is the day after the full moon. I gather the flowers, removing the stamens from them.

After making the essence, I bottle it and stabilize two of the quarts. Just when I begin stabilizing the third quart, it starts to rain with small round bits of hail in the rain. The crystals and bamboo board get a bit muddy, but I proceed with the stabilization process, and complete it without problems.

The day before making the essence, I had hung around the campsite for a few hours, waiting for the person camped there to return. The site was labeled for departure that day. When she returned and was gathering her things, I asked her if I could move into the site when she left. She curtly said, "You'll have to wait 'til I'm out" or some other abrupt words to that effect.

The next day, right before the rain, I meet an older woman at a nearby campsite and I tell her about making the essence. She says she'd like to have some. I tell her I have a small amount left over and will bring her some. She says it is good that I will bring it to her because she has hurt her hip and can't walk well. When I return, I tell her to think about her hip while taking the essence. I stand behind her and help her focus on her hip while she takes it.

The next day, I run into the first lady at a bookstore in town. She apologizes for having been somewhat curt at the campground and says that her friend has told her how I helped her hip.

This story makes me reflect on how much we all, myself included, judge people on their externals. This lady was curt to someone who to her didn't look "special," but after finding out that I have some quality she respects, she apologizes and wants to interact with me. I want to remember this and to go forward realizing that each of us is a magnificent spirit and not judge.

Two days after the bookstore meeting, I relate the story of the two women I met to a friend. Then I say, "I don't know why I told you this story."

My friend says, "I know. It is because one of the gifts of slender penstemon is non-judgment."

THE ESSENCE AND THE LABEL

The cover of a book is our first hint as to its contents. When we see a book cover on a shelf, coffee table, or computer screen, we quickly decide whether the book has any relevance to our own life. We are attracted, repelled, or disinterested instantly.

The label of a flower essence is like the cover of a book. It immediately communicates an indefinable message about the contents of the bottle. When people see the bottle or a box of bottles on the shelf, they will immediately be attracted, repelled, or disinterested, depending on the relevance to their own lives of the vibration that's being communicated by the artwork. Flower essences that have been grown or wild harvested by me and created by me in partnership with Nature carry my vibration in addition to their own. This is the vibration that must be communicated through the label.

I'm no artist, but luckily my friend Zara has the capacity to translate my vibration and the vibration of the flower essence line I'm creating into paint. Her luminous painting will be the background for the flower essence labels and will immediately communicate some sense of my vibration to all who see them. In this way, those who can most benefit from the essences will be drawn to buy them.

I feel that in creating this line of essences, I am drawing on all my past history and accomplishments, known and unknown. I'm using all my intellect, intuition, and alliances in their creation. I thank all the people and entities, embodied and discarnate, who are helping me. My heartfelt gratitude goes out to them all.

CHAPTER 7

A JOURNEY TO PERU

My friend Kalia, our shaman from the Mimzy Project, has decided to sign up for a tour of Peru organized by her friend Cheryl. Cheryl goes to Peru often, and once a year brings a group of North Americans to visit the sacred sites in the Andes. Kalia's friend Devora, who was a tether for the Mimzy Project, will also be going.

In my view, going anywhere with Kalia is a good idea, and the prospect of a tour of the sacred sites of Peru is too delicious to pass up. I tell Skidmore that I'm going to Peru with Kalia and ask him if he'd like to come. I'm happy when he says yes. I know that doing ceremony at sacred sites is not really Skidmore's thing, but I also know that he'll be happy traveling with the group and that we will enjoy his sociability.

On October 31, 2011, Skidmore and I fly to Houston, where we spend the night at a friend's home before flying to Lima on All Saints' Day. In Lima, after a couple of hours of making our way through customs, we find ourselves in a huge waiting room filled with hundreds of people. We're in a large, long, roped-off runway. On the other side of the ropes are crowded multitudes of tour guides, each holding a sign indicating the name of a tour group or the name of a person they are there to meet. Finally we find a young man holding the sign for Cheryl's tour. He escorts us to a seating area where other tour members are waiting. Devora is there and introduces herself to us.

We arrive at the hotel after midnight. I'm touched because Kalia is still up, waiting for us and for Devora. It's been a year and a half since that painful day I said goodbye to her in the City of Mount Shasta, and I'm thrilled to be with her again and starting another adventure.

On November 2, we fly from Lima to Cusco. A tour bus takes us from there to our lodgings in Urubamba, in the area of Peru known as the Sacred Valley. We'll stay at the beautiful Monasterio de la Recoleta for four nights. The first night we begin the ceremonial part of our tour with a fire ceremony conducted by a shaman. The shaman calls in the six directions: north, south, east, west, above, and below. He anoints each of our foreheads with an essential oil, and my third eye vibrates to his touch.

The next day we drive through incredible scenery. The Andean region is somewhat barren, with few trees, so the mountains and gigantic boulders are stark against the sky. We arrive at a school near Pachar. Many of the children walk two hours each way down narrow treks from their homes in the mountains above to attend this school. We hand out gifts and school supplies that we have brought to give to the kids.

Later, we drive to Moray, where we meet a Q'ero shaman and priest, Lorenzo, and his wife, Maria. The Q'ero have lived for centuries in remote villages high in the Andes. Now the Q'ero shamans say that this is the time they are destined to come down from their villages to share their teachings with other Peruvians and the many seekers from other countries who are visiting Peru.

Moray is the site of an ancient energy vortex. This vortex was enhanced by the Incas, who were presumably encouraged and guided by beings that assisted them in building all their sacred sites. The land at Moray forms a natural bowl. This bowl was developed by the Incas into concentric circles of terraces that pull energy into the bowl and spiral it down into the final circle below. We follow the path of the energy, walking around the circular terraces and gradually moving downward until we also reach the center circle. Here the energy leaves the surface of the earth, continuing to ground itself deep within.

Later, on nearby terraces, Lorenzo performs a traditional Q'ero ceremony. During the ceremony, I feel as though the ground is moving in waves. Kalia is aware that many ancestors are present for the ceremony.

Later, I buy a beautiful Q'ero mesa, or altar, cloth from Lorenzo. My Nature team had told me before we left for Peru that I was to look for a cloth made by the Q'ero for use in the making of my flower essences. The Q'ero now dye most of their hand-woven cloth with bright synthetic dyes because they're popular and sell well. But the altar cloth I buy is richly colored with traditional native plant dyes in geometric patterns in subdued brown, black, and blue.

The next day we drive to another school, also for Quechua students, high in the Andes. On the way, we stop at a place where several small waterfalls are running down the mountain side and into a stream. Here we hold a water ceremony. I have brought several stones and crystals from home that tested as wanting to come with me to Peru. One of these is the red, heart-shaped rock I found on Pfeiffer Beach at Big Sur. This rock tests as wanting to stay here in this mountain stream.

I send love into the rock, and then toss it into the stream, energetically connecting this land with Big Sur.

When we arrive at the school, some of the teachers, students and parents are making lunch for us. Our tour guide company sponsors projects to benefit children in the Andean villages. The project at this site includes greenhouses to grow produce for lunches. The plants in the greenhouse are simple herbs and vegetables that appear to be vibrant with health. They were picked that day, then immediately cooked. Our lunch is a delicious quinoa and herb soup with potatoes and herb tea.

Next we visit the ancient site of Ollantaytambo on the Urubamba River. Here 50-ton andesite boulders have been brought from distant quarries and perfectly fitted together using some ancient technology unknown to us. There is an extensive system of aqueducts and fountains, which still function. We walk past the fountains to find a vantage point from which to view the part-natural, part-carved figure of a condor high on the mountain across the river from us.

From this vantage point, a shaman leads us in a meditation on the condor. Incan prophesy says that when the condor (representing the peoples of South America) flies with the eagle (representing the peoples of North America), there will be peace on Earth.

After the meditation, we climb the terraces and find ourselves on the back side of the site overlooking fields in a valley below. Our guide grew up here; these terraces were his childhood playground. Kalia asks him, "There is a civilization below the mountain, isn't there?" He nods. She tells him that she sensed there was a city under the ground because the energy feels similar to that of Mount Shasta with its underground city in North America. We spend some moments connecting with those beneath the mountain, sending them our love. Then we sit for a time in blissful peace with the sun warming us.

The sites of Moray and Ollantaytambo have confirmed to me that these places are not mere architectural ruins. They are powerful vortices of energy strongly conveying incoming energy into the global grid. Unlike some vortices that I have visited in the United States, they don't seem to need bolstering or cleansing. If their power was ever diminished in the past, they have clearly been reactivated since then and are operating at full power in our present time.

The next day, November 5, is our last day at the beautiful Monasterio de la Recoleta.

Our tour bus brings us to the village of Pisaq. We drive through the town and up the mountain to the Incan site above. Shaman Carlos leads us in a cleansing ceremony at the temple that is known as the Temple of the Falcon. After the ceremony, we want to climb the mountain to visit the temple at the top, but we don't have much time before our bus leaves to take us to lunch in town.

Kalia and Devora especially want to make it to the top because Kalia says the temple has been and is currently in use by the bird tribe, a tribe of bird-people who inhabit a nearby dimension, and their energies can be felt here.

We begin racing up the mountain, but I get sick in the blaring sun on the way up. Kalia stops to pump energy into me, and I feel better. But I need to stop. I clearly can't continue to the top of the mountain.

Skidmore finds us, and I tell Kalia to go ahead, that Skidmore will take care of me. But Kalia doesn't want to leave me. I'm almost in tears because I'm sure I'll be okay and I don't want Kalia to miss the opportunity to visit the bird temple.

Finally Marty, one of our guides, arrives and leads us to a place in the shade where Skidmore can stay with me until the others return. Kalia then leaves, but later I find out that she wasn't able to make it to the top in time. Devora did, though. She ran as though she were flying as she was magnetically and effortlessly drawn to the top of the mountain.

That afternoon, we do our Christmas shopping in the famous Pisaq open-air market with its rows of stalls selling colorful Peruvian handicrafts. We buy soft woven Alpaca scarves, tooled leather wallets, handmade leather slippers lined with fleece, and shell necklaces imported from the coast to give to our friends and family.

The next day we take a train to Aguas Calientes, the closest town to Machu Picchu. The train is the only access to the town other than by foot. Almost all the tourists and all food and supplies are brought in by rail. Those who hike in are following the ancient trail built by the Incas to access Machu Picchu. The hike typically takes two or four days depending on the starting point. Hikers experience ancient Inca ruins, high mountain passes, foggy cloud forests and orchid-rich jungles before passing through the Sun Gate with its magnificent view of Machu Picchu below.

I'm still not well, but I'm hoping to be better tomorrow for the most anticipated day of the tour: our visit to Machu Picchu.

I have another problem that's been brewing for some time. I've been trying to ignore it, but it's clear that our tour group leader, Cheryl, doesn't like me . . . or Skidmore. She's critical of much of what I say and do, and I've just been letting it slide off me. Now it seems that there is a misunderstanding about choices of activities for tomorrow. Cheryl refuses to let me come with Kalia to an initiation.

Devora suggests that I work with earth energies during the time that Kalia is in the initiation. Cheryl's attitude is getting to me until Kalia points out that spiritual teachers often can be harsh in their behavior, and when they are, it's usually not personal. This reframing of the situation expands my viewpoint and I feel better.

After lunch, Kalia and I hang out in the restaurant long after the others have left, drinking tea and talking. It's the first long talk I've had alone with her during the trip, and it is the highlight of my day. That evening I stay in bed instead of going to dinner. Skidmore brings me two small slices of pizza.

MACHU PICCHU, THE CRYSTAL CITY

On awakening in the morning, I attempt to psychically offer Cheryl a truce. Many of those on the tour are her students, so she tends to talk to me as if I'm one of them. All I want is for her to recognize that she's not my teacher and I'm not her student, so she can just ignore me and we'll be fine. After I psychically offer this information to her, as an invitation to establish an energetic truce, she immediately attacks me energetically three times on my sacrum. The three hits are instantaneous and stinging like strikes from a scorpion's tail. I have to quickly call down strength from my higher self to my physical body in order defend myself. I'm shocked and amazed by the speed and intensity of her attack.

After an early breakfast, we take one of the buses to the site of Machu Picchu. The steep, narrow road with switchbacks up the side of the mountain gives us spectacular views of the cloud forest and valley below.

I've seen many pictures and videos of Machu Picchu, but nothing prepares me for the intensity of the energy I feel once there. I'm walking along the path to the site with Devora when we turn a corner, and suddenly Machu Picchu appears below me. I have an overwhelming sense of recognition when I first see the city. My heart overflows and I begin sobbing. Devora looks at me and says, "Welcome back."

Through my tears, I manage to quip, "Thanks, it's been a while."

Devora can remember a life when she did music therapy for the people of the city from atop Huayna Picchu, a tall mountain across from the main site of Machu Picchu.

At one point in our tour of the city, I find a niche in the rock and I sit down inside it. It feels strangely familiar and Devora says, "That's your niche." Since I'm not going to the initiation, it seems I will have extra time to return to this niche. So that I can find my way back, I ask our guide, Eduardo, to show me where we are on my map of Machu Picchu.

Hearing my question, Cheryl starts haranguing me, telling me I'm selfish to interrupt Eduardo's meditation. I say, "I'm sorry Eduardo, if I interrupted your meditation," and I begin walking away, putting my map in my back pocket. But Cheryl continues haranguing me, so I turn back toward her and make a clearing and protective motion with my arm, saying, "Cheryl, I decline to accept."

Cheryl shrugs her shoulders and I move away, but this is a pivotal moment for me. I've publically recognized the tension between us, and I've told her that I won't accept her harassment. But I'm not attacking her or arguing with her either.

Later, Cheryl implies I cut in line waiting for the "I take my power back" seat. This is a stone seat that we are each to sit on, holding a hiking pole like a scepter while saying, "I take my power back." I actually didn't want to do this exercise, and said something else inside myself, something like, "This is my domain; my power is strong within me."

Skidmore actually refuses to say Cheryl's phrase, telling Cheryl that he can't take his power back because he never gave it away. Cheryl disagrees, telling him, "Yes, you did."

Before lunch, I climb up some terraces and sit facing the peak that in translation means "Happy Mountain." I meditate, letting my spirits sink deeply into this familiar feeling place. This is not the first time I have sat on these terraces in meditation!

A few llamas are nearby, doing their job of keeping the grass on the terraces trimmed. I gather three pinches of sand, placing each in its own envelope. The envelopes are for me, Zara, and my brother-in-law, Matt. I take the stone I found on Lake Siskiyou with Zara. It wants to stay here, so I throw it over the nearby steps onto a terrace from where it bounces down to a lower terrace and disappears into the grass.

After lunch a group of us climb to the Sun Gate with Marty as our guide. On our way, I meet a flower that I'd like to make a flower essence from. It's violet with tiny flowers forming a cone, and with large, broad, heavily veined leaves.

As I continue hiking the steep path toward the Sun Gate, I decide to shift my approach to Cheryl again. The next time she harangues me, I'm prepared to say to her, "Cheryl, let's get together someday in a later life, have a beer, and laugh about it." But it turns out that I never have to actually say it. Apparently, getting to the place within myself where it's all a big joke was all that was needed. After that, she treats me decently for the rest of the trip, and even makes an occasional friendly remark to me.

After arriving at the Sun Gate and enjoying the magnificent view of the Crystal City below, I walk through the gate and take a seat on the ground overlooking the other side of the mountain. Hikers are walking up the Inca Trail towards us, headed for the Sun Gate and the mystical city that lies beyond and beneath it.

When walking back from the Sun Gate, I apparently miss the turn and end up on the stairs between the terraces where I had meditated before. Marty apparently thought he needed to find me, and we both end up meeting Devora and Kalia at the bottom of the terraces. Devora shows me her photo of Skidmore leaning out, arms spread wide into nothingness, at the top of Huayna Picchu with Roberto, one of our guides, holding him.

That night we sit with Devora at dinner and order pizza. After dinner, Skidmore goes to the hot springs with the others, but I go back to the hotel to get a good night's sleep.

I realize that I've been tested that day, and that I passed the test. I know that the discomfort between Cheryl and me probably goes back to another lifetime, possibly even to a lifetime at Machu Picchu. Whatever the cause, I found the key to the solution of the problem. My first idea, to decline abuse without attacking or blaming was good, but not enough to ease the tension. The key was humor. That and the recognition that, in the end, when all roles are played out, all souls are friends and united in the One.

Although I had tried to tell Cheryl that she is not my teacher, I end up being taught an important lesson through her.

CUSCO
The next morning we leave Aguas Calientes, taking the

train back to Cusco. At the hotel we check into next, I'm exhausted and nap until dinner. I'm grateful that I felt well the day before when visiting Manchu Picchu, but now the weakness and traveler's diarrhea has returned. We dine in a restaurant with a floor show with native dancers and musicians. It's clear that our guides are enjoying the performance of the female dancers in their low-cut, short dresses.

Skidmore is chosen to dance on stage with the performers. They put a long, narrow strip of cloth through his belt behind his back. Then they dance around him with lighters, trying to set his "tail" on fire. Everyone is laughing and cheering them on and Skidmore is a great sport about it.

The next day is our second and last day in Cusco. Our tour bus takes us to the sacred site of Saqsaywaman. The site's walls are made of huge boulders, perfectly cut and rounded. These boulders are fitted so closely together that no mortar is needed and a piece of paper can't be slid between them. We meditate at one of the towering walls, each of us with our body flat against a massive boulder.

After this meditation, I notice that Devora's aura is so high that she's shaking. I offer to help ground her, holding her and sending our combined energies into the earth. Her energy stabilizes and she feels better. I'm happy that I could do something for her since she's helped me so much with her grace and generosity of spirit.

I'm still weak and the sun's heat is oppressive. I call in my White Brotherhood MAP team to help me in the sun. After working with them for a time, I feel stronger.

The shaman Sebastian does a lovely music therapy ceremony for us. After the ceremony, Skidmore gives Sebastian an offering, but doesn't buy a copy of the CD that Sebastian is selling. However, Sebastian insists that we take a CD as a gift "to remember him."

I'm too sick to eat much of the picnic lunch and on our return to the hotel, I spend the rest of the afternoon and evening in bed. I have the chills and intense diarrhea, so I take a homeopathic remedy and have two more MAP sessions.

PUNO

The next day, we drive by bus all day to reach Puno, a city in southeastern Peru that is on the shore of Lake Titicaca. We break at Raqchi, an ancient Inca sanctuary with high stone walls like totems. Each wall is split from the next by a thin, but not straight, divide. The effect is as if the walls were one huge sheet of paper with cracks torn out of it. In a circular stone room with a thatched roof, the group starts chanting, "Om." I become dizzy and have to leave to lie outside flat on the ground. My intestines are too shaky and I'm too sick to be sending out energy through my upper chakras.

We arrive at our Puno hotel. Our room on the eighth floor has a magnificent view of Lake Titicaca with the full moon shining on it. The whole group dines at a restaurant with another floor show. Devora, Skidmore, and I have pizza again. The three of us, plus Kalia, are sitting near the guides, who are again enjoying watching scantily dressed female dancers. The highlight of the floor show this evening is an amazing bird dance performed by three male dancers with elaborate and strange bird masks and feathers.

That night, Kalia psychically asks the ETs to wake us when they are near. I don't know about this until later, but I snap awake at 4:30 a.m., the same time as Devora and Kalia.

Amara Muro's Door, November 11, 2011

Today is the day known as Eleven Eleven Eleven. It's a day of worldwide ceremony. I awaken early in my hotel room. The rising sun is casting a reddish-pink glow on the mountains, which is reflected by the calm waters of Lake Titicaca below. Today our group is traveling to the sacred site of Amara Muro's portal. I'm excited as I picture myself there with Skidmore and my beloved friends Kalia and Devora.

Legend tells the story of Amara Muro, a priest. At the time of the sinking of Lemuria, he brought a sacred golden sun disk from a Lemurian temple and placed it for safe keeping in a hidden place deep below the waters of Lake Titicaca. Later he left our world, not through the usual doorway of death, but by entering a portal into a star gate and beyond. This is the portal we are to visit today.

Our bus pulls off the road near the site around 7 a.m. Some would see this area as barren, for there are scarcely any trees. Instead huge sandstone boulders dramatically define the landscape and the horizon. We walk up a fairly steep trail to the site itself. The face of a massive sandstone outcropping has been carved flat so that it presents a towering vertical wall. In the center of that wall, on a ledge above the ground, is a recessed alcove that looks like a doorway. On each side of the doorway, a few steps along the ledge, are carved half-circular niches that reach all the way up to the top of the towering wall. This site has been revered by the indigenous people of Peru for several millennia.

Our group begins taking turns experiencing the small niches and the doorway. Upon my turn, I climb onto the ledge and walk into the first niche. I face into the sandstone with my back to the group and ask for cleansing, as I've been told is the custom. I'm not sure I feel cleansing in particular, but I do feel connected to the rock and to this ancient place that carries a spirit of timelessness.

Then I move into the portal itself, placing the front of my body against the rock and holding my arms open wide, inviting in whatever vibrations might be coming through the rock from the star gate beyond. I feel a mystical connection to all, as is normal for me to feel in a sacred time at a sacred space.

As I move into the second niche, I ask that the experience be integrated into my cellular body so that I may access it whenever desired. Then I climb down from the ledge and join my husband and friends sitting on the ground below.

The area where we are sitting is flat and ringed with small boulders, forming a sitting area for groups using the site. On the other side of the ring of boulders, the ground drops away to a much larger and roughly circular plain below. As we have been sitting there, many groups of people have been arriving in vans and tour buses for the ceremony soon to come.

The area is filling with people and many are grouping themselves on the plain below. Some are carrying banners identifying their groups. Some are dressed all in white with flowers in their hair. There are African and Peruvian shamans dressed in their regional native garments. This ceremony was originally planned for 200 people, and more than 400 have arrived.

The conductor of the ceremony, Jorge Luis Delgado, arrives. I've read his book *Andean Awakening* and I recognize him from the pictures in the book. From reading the book, I know that he is a shaman. He begins addressing the crowd in Spanish, repeating everything in English. He asks all those who are 60 years old or more to come forward to take the lead in forming a line. All the elders, including Skidmore and me, hold hands.

Then he has all the shamans come forward and take their places on the ledge above us. There are shamans from all over the world. Cheryl and Frances from our group are two of these. Roberto, one of our guides, is also one. Some shamans are clearly Peruvian, some are Anglos, and some are African.

Everyone else has now joined hands also, the elders first, followed by all the others, forming a long line that switches back through the upper area and down onto the plain below. The first person in this long line is the woman to my right. She sits on a huge rock under the portal and is clearly grounding the line. I hold her left hand with my right, also supporting the grounding. Skidmore is on my left, then all the remaining elders. From my vantage point at the top of the line, I have a magnificent view of all the people below and also of the shamans on the ledge above.

Delgado addresses the crowd again in Spanish, repeating his remarks in English. He talks about love, service, and wisdom, the three Incan laws I remember from his book. After he speaks, each of the shamans gives an invocation from his or her own tradition in his or her own traditional language.

Then all of us, still holding hands, start to move down the snake-like switchbacks, carrying the energy created above down into the field below. Meanwhile, those below are compressing their lines into a tightly wound spiral of people. This coordinated and intentional motion of people of all nationalities, races, and religions moves me profoundly. I'm not alone. I see many others with uplifted auras and tears of joy glistening in their eyelashes.

Finally we all arrive in one tight spiral on the plain below. We have moved the energy of the portal and the shamans, spiraling it down to the circular plain. Delgado addresses the crowd again, completing the ceremony. Then people begin turning to each other, hugging one another. For about ten minutes, we all mill around, each hugging as many of the others as we can. Everyone is in an ecstatic space of love and gratitude.

Later, we eat a boxed lunch at a nearby high area around the hill from the main site. It's backed by dramatic hills with magnificent high boulders and has a panoramic view of the expanse below.

I've been asking the tour guides to take us to the shore of the lake so that we can touch the water. On the way back to Puno, they take us to a place near Jorge Luis Delgado's Puno hotel. From there, we can walk down a lane and make our way to the edge of the water.

This part of the lake is quite muddy and full of weeds. Before leaving home, we had been told to bring an item to Peru to throw away, an item representing something that we wanted out of our lives, so we bring it to Peru to leave it there. I had created a collage representing limitation. I silently tear up the collage and toss the fragments into the muddy water, symbolically releasing my sense of limitation to the sacred portal of the lake. I use kinesiology to test my crystals and throw in two of them that want to stay there. Our guide tells us that if we ever come back to Puno, we can take a boat to the reed islands and maybe even sleep on one of them. I want to do this!

That evening, we enjoy a slide show of the photos that the photographer of our guide company has taken. He presents memory sticks of the photos to us as gifts. After the slide show, we have dinner in the hotel restaurant and do another meditation before bed. We have to be up at 5:30 the next morning to leave the hotel at 7:00 a.m. for our flight to Lima.

That night I silently ask the ETs to wake me when they arrive. I'm taking a page from Kalia's book because when she did this the night before, she had been awakened at 11:15 p.m., and later at 4:30 a.m. This night, I jolt out of sleep at 11:15 p.m., my whole body vibrating so intensely that the bed is shaking. I look at the Lake, but I see no lightning or UFOs, so I quickly return to sleep.

GOODBYE

On our last day in Peru, the sunrise over the lake is a pearly luminescence. We drive to the Juliaca airport and fly to Lima. Then we are taken to a hotel in the suburb of Milleflores. We only have about four hours before leaving again for the Lima airport.

Skidmore and I walk along the ocean parkway and discover a huge modern shopping mall filled with affluent stores and people. This is a different Peru than the one we have lived in for the past ten days.

After our ocean walk, I rest until it's time to leave for the airport. Kalia, Devora, Skidmore, and I, along with several others, are being bussed to the airport together. Cheryl is in the lobby saying goodbye to those leaving. I give her a quick hug and tell her goodbye. She responds with a quick hug back. I get on the bus and tell Devora that I hugged Cheryl goodbye. I feel proud of myself, because I always took the high road in my interactions with Cheryl. Devora says she is proud of me, too, and I feel the satisfaction of a job well done and getting acknowledgement for it.

There is so much crowding and activity at the Lima airport that I don't get a chance to say a proper goodbye to Devora and Kalia. I hold them in my heart and I have to believe that I will see them again soon.

CHAPTER 8

MY TRUE HOME

In the final days of 2011, Skidmore and I start a new diet, called the Metabolic Balance Diet. Our blood is drawn at a clinic and sent for analysis and our medical history is taken. Based on the results, we each receive a personalized list of foods and amounts to choose from. In my journal, I question my guides about the diet and its significance. I write down their answers as best I can.

METABOLIC BALANCE DIET:
JOURNAL ENTRY, JANUARY 4, 2012

Question: How is this diet working through me?

Answer: A change was needed and you needed a vehicle to get it done. With your old structure of eating, you would never make permanent progress. You need body vitality to do the work ahead. The body you had could have been transformed just by the action of light. But as soon as you consumed another meal based on old habits and easy availability, you would find the action of the light being canceled by the action of the food. So a way to get your attention as to the quality and quantity of your food was needed. This diet allows you to develop sensitivity to what you are eating, while enforcing a pattern of healthy eating.

During this time, you are developing a different expectation and experience of what healthy eating actually is for you. You are also developing a greater appreciation for the differences in foods.

Just like your beloved flower essences, each food carries a different energetic pattern. So even though you think of kale, chard, and bok choy as fulfilling the same needs of the body, they are not the same, and are not perceived as the same by your body. You have a tendency to think, *It doesn't matter what I eat as long as it's healthy and as long as I get enough vitamins, minerals, and proteins.* As a homeopath, you will know better once you allow yourself to see that small amounts of phytochemicals really do make a difference. And that the phytochemicals themselves are a result of the energetic pattern of the plant or animal as created by the archetype of that being.

Allow yourself to take in the loving and nurturing energy of each food as you eat it. At the appropriate time, as your diet allows, you will develop the discernment to experience which plant and animal foods are sustaining and enlivening to you, and which are not.

The other way the diet is helping you is through its action on your husband. He needed this change even more than you, and he also needs body vitality to sustain him during the times ahead. The partnership between you will grow and strengthen as a result of the two of you meeting this challenge together. Together you have much good to do in the world. Your increased bodily vitality will allow you to continue to do good work even while aging.

As you eat, consciously focus on what is happening: how your body is taking energy solidified into food, unlocking it, and turning it into energy again. Yes, some of it remains, becoming part of the cells of your body, but much of it becomes energy again. The more light there is in the food you are eating, the more enlightened the cells of your body can become.

As your cells enlighten, the more crystalline the structure of your body becomes. And the more crystalline your body becomes, the more you can interact with realms hidden to you now. It's important that you learn these truths through direct experience. Only through direct experience can you gain a deeper knowledge that can be convincingly imparted to others.

RESULTS

Soon after writing the above journal entry, I started to notice increased energy due to the changes in my eating. I ended up losing 25 pounds on the plan and loving my lighter, thinner body. And my new clothes!

THE REALM OF THE WILD AND THE SWEET

I walk out of my house, across the covered wooden porch, and down two wooden steps to the concrete sidewalk. Emerging from underneath the porch roof, I check out the sky, getting my first feeling for the day, whether it is bright or gray. I pass raised beds on my left, maneuver myself through the cumbersome gate, and walk toward the chicken coop.

Raised beds, clunky gate, chicken coop—each is a point of endeavor, an outcome of my love and labor, and that of my husband. We are ushering in life, but we're not doing it alone. Unseen companions work with us daily. I walk down the drive a ways, then circle around past the greenhouse and down an incline to the firebreak road below. I'm entering the realm of the wild and the sweet, now being transformed into a more manicured wildness by my husband, who is clearing it according to the instructions of our unseen friends.

As I walk into this realm, I see how uncovered it now is. The rocks are uncovered and you can see their magnificent formations. You can now trace descending pathways where the water flows when it rains. An ancient tree spirit can be glimpsed in an old, twisted, red-barked manzanita tree. And the land is rejoicing in these changes and calling for more, calling for more clearing and calling for the bees. The bees are a necessity now; the land and I are trying to be patient waiting for them. As the bees stabilize themselves here, a new order will snap into place with a satisfying click.

Our Nature spirit companions have further plans for this land. I can only sketch the outlines of their plans, can only catch glimpses of what they are creating and why. Part of their plan requires adjusting the mineral structure of the soil. They know some way of transmuting the soil into a form that better suits their intentions. I was told by two human experts that we should not have removed the buckbrush, because the buckbrush fixes nitrogen in the soil. But Nature clearly wanted them gone. There was something about them energetically that no longer benefits this land.

I know that soil can be transformed by using energy. If you spray homeopathic silica on the land, you will affect water retention and the soil will become either moister or drier. With soil balancing techniques, you can change the structure of soil faster and easier than with fertilizer alone. I think there is a way to energetically detoxify land that has been misused so that it can be made fertile again. This is the way of the future. This is what I want to learn more about and to share the knowledge with others.

FROM THE PWN HANDBOOK

My winter garden in 2012 is small, one raised bed for winter vegetables—chard, kale, broccoli, lettuce, arugula, bok choy—and another raised bed just for garlic. In most of the other beds I'll rake in clover seeds for a cover crop, leaving one last bed for spring wildflowers.

A garden is an easily understood example of the relationship I call partnering with Nature. It's clear that a garden is not just Nature operating on its own. That would be an untrammeled Amazon jungle, a dense forest, or an endless grass prairie. It's also clear that we humans cannot grow a garden on our own without Nature. Even the most highly manipulated GM crop, grown with petroleum-based fertilizer, still requires Nature's processes to live. Therefore, all gardens are the result of a partnership with Nature.

Perhaps because gardens are the quintessential partnership with Nature, Nature intelligence itself has used the word "garden" to refer to any partnership projects between humans and Nature. Using the word in this way, Yosemite Park becomes a garden. We think of it as a wilderness, but actually humans have created the park boundaries and have determined the purpose of the park. It's an excellent illustration of how humans and Nature can best work together in creating a garden.

Humans decide the boundaries of the garden and its intent, direction, and purpose. Nature puts in place processes to fulfill that direction and purpose, and will organize and unfold these processes in such a way that a magnificent balance is continually maintained. By clearly defining the direction and purpose of the garden, and by consulting with Nature about each step of implementation and maintenance, we humans can create the most productive gardens with Nature.

If any partnership projects with Nature can be called a garden, then any project that we humans carry out in the physical world also is a garden. Because Nature is in charge of form, any use of form involves partnering with Nature. This includes any use of our bodies, which are our physical forms. Writing a book is creating a garden. Building a bird house is creating a garden. We are creating gardens whether or not we are conscious of it.

If we give a project a name, definition, and purpose, and if we request Nature's assistance and consult with Nature intelligence at each step, then we have a garden created in conscious partnership with Nature, a garden that has more opportunity to be productive and bountiful—and one that will bring us more pleasure and gratitude.

CRACK THE CODE: JOURNAL ENTRY, JANUARY 18, 2012
"There is a crack in everything. That's how the light gets in."
—Leonard Cohen

Crack the code. I want to crack entrenched codes. So many such codes are already cracked; now they're *wabi-sabi* codes with light streaming through them.

Two hundred years ago, Samuel Hahnemann, the discoverer of homeopathy, cracked the entrenched code that said that medicine needs to contain a physical substance in order to have a physical effect on the body. In the 20th century, the Findhorn community cracked the entrenched code that said that the only elements needed for a plant to grow are physical ones: seed, soil, sun, and water.

A flower essence creator tells me that the negative effects of a barcode on a flower essence bottle can't be mitigated energetically—not by the color of the barcode, or by a genesa crystal, or by any other energetic technique. He says, therefore, to seek a physical solution. For example, put your product's barcode on a box containing the bottle, or leave the barcode off altogether. To seek an energetic solution to an energetic problem, and to actually believe the solution will work, he ascribes as "wishful thinking."

The world we are entering does not work by the same rules as the world we are leaving behind us. To see our new world more clearly, we have to discard, disregard, cancel, and refuse to believe in the old code, the old rules.

One night I was sitting in my hot tub, watching streaks of red glowing in the sunset sky. I started to receive a download. Since I didn't know whom I was receiving it from, I stopped it for a moment. I quickly connected to entities I know well and trust to protect me, then reopened to receive the transmission. Energy flowed in from above and streamed down into the left side of my body.

I knew this energy was information, but I didn't know how to understand or decode it with my mind. I decided that I wanted to receive it into the right side of my body as well, so I started diverting part of the download stream into the right side. After a few moments, I was able to balance the stream so that it was entering both sides of my body equally. I was hoping that by having some right-sided access to it, I would be able to decipher it better with my conscious mind.

However, that did not happen. Yet I have some sense of what this information was about. The information that was downloaded into my body had relevance to the renewal of our planet, relevance to how we can use energy to transform physical form.

I immediately wanted to bring this information out of the opacity with which I saw it. I wanted to break the code that was preventing me from knowing it more clearly, the code of my belief that said that either this information couldn't be known or couldn't be true, or that I was not a person who could know it. However, I estimated that my realization of this information was already a done deal and couldn't be prevented. Therefore I placed my faith in my future knowing with the assurance that this was *not* wishful thinking.

WRITING

I knew for a couple of years that I would be doing some kind of writing beyond my journal. I knew for several months that I would be writing a book entitled *Partnering with Nature*. In early February 2012, I worked with an editor on an outline for the book. The book, as I conceived it back then, was more of a how-to book than the book you are currently reading.

I wrote part of a chapter, and sent it to the editor. When she edited it and sent it back to me, I was perplexed. Most of her suggested edits improved the wording, making the text smoother to read. But some of them left me with the feeling that the book I was writing was not the book that she was editing. I didn't realize then that I was trying to write the wrong book.

I didn't know what to do about this, but I told myself that I didn't have to figure it out right now. It was early spring and time for me to be wild harvesting desert plants and creating flower essences.

Brittlebush and Creosote Bush

In March, Skidmore, our dog Skip, and I embark on another road trip. South of Joshua Tree National Park, I gather and create flower essences from creosote bush (*Larrea tridentata*) and brittlebush (*Encelia farinosa*). Before gathering flowers, I always ask the plant for permission to take them for the making of an essence. I expect the plant to respond with a yes, because that is almost always what happens. Today, I'm surprised when I receive a no from the first Brittlebush plant I ask.

I walk around that area of the desert, finding Brittlebush plants and asking them if I can use a few of their blossoms to make an essence for the healing of humans. Most of the Brittlebush plants are unwilling, but I finally find a couple of willing plants, enough to make the essence I need. My impression is that these plants are not concerned about human needs—a completely understandable feeling.

Deep Creek

As John O'Donohue said, your soul knows the geography of your destiny. And really there's nowhere to go, because wholeness *is*. Wholeness shines as an ineffable light within me and you, and within every plant and rock on our planet. There are just blocks in the way that keep me from seeing it. The blocks are within me. I look at the blocks, I see them and I get stuck. My life feels like a vacillation between wholeness and stuckness. Each day presents the question, "Which one will show itself today?"

The day we hike to Deep Creek is a day unblocked. We pack our lunch and leave our small RV, taking Skip with us. Skip is thrilled to be out in the fresh air, hiking through the dry, scrubby landscape, sniffing low-growing plants and looking for lizards. Many plants are ones also found growing near our home, like buckbrush and manzanita.

The path descends as we switch back closer to the canyon and the river. Suddenly I experience a shift. The field changes as we enter the realm of the rock and other Nature spirits. These spirits are around us always, but we have just entered one of their special domains. And because this is an unblocked day, I am lifted out of the normal confines of self and into an awareness of their immanent presence. I feel myself expand to encompass the gigantic rock figures around me, and the river and canyon below. Oh happy day! To be free of the small "I" and expand into the greater "I am."

Once we reach the river, I lie on the sandy bank while Skidmore crosses through the water to reach the hot springs on the other side. Lying in the sunshine with Skip at my side, I feel the warmth of the sand supporting my back. I experience the sand as a repository that welcomes all the negative feelings and limitations that I can deposit there. I know that the earth can take any dead, stuck, or blocked energy and cleanse it and release it to freely continue its journey. So I allow the magic of the moment to work its way with me and release all the negativity I can access into the sand.

After experiencing this precious release, I arc energy from where I am lying back into the vortex on our home property. I do this to stabilize the experience so that I can access some of the magnificence of this place once I've returned to my normal daily life.

After a time, my husband returns. We eat our lunch and then begin the long hike climbing out of the canyon. As I hike, I keep turning to look back, maintaining connection with the Nature spirits of the place. Finally we come to what I know is the boundary of their special domain. I look back one last time, sending them my love and gratitude before slowly turning away.

Pygmy Cedar, Arroyo Willow, Pincushion Flower, and Oriental Poppy

I gather pygmy cedar (*Peucephyllum schottii*) flowers in the morning from a wash near the Shamanic Valley Campground. The plant has a sticky resin and needle-like leaves and smells like cedar.

Three days later, I gather catkins of arroyo willow (*Salix lasiolepis*) near a mountain stream. The willows seem joyous with spring energy.

I return home, and a week later, on Easter Sunday, I make a pincushion flower (*Scabiosa columbaria*) essence from flowers I have grown from the seed.

On May Day, I make an Oriental poppy (*Papaver orientale*) essence from flowers that I had planted from seedlings the previous fall.

From the PWN Handbook

I've been asked to give a talk about sacred plants, but I don't know how to distinguish particular plants as "sacred." To me, all plants are sacred plants. Their sacredness is in our perception, not in their reality.

Every time we inhale, we breathe in oxygen they have released. Every time we eat, we nourish ourselves with plants or with animals who have nourished their bodies with plants. Every time we grieve, they take our released emotion and work to balance it. The plants attend to us constantly, adapting subtly to our energy whatever we do, wherever we go. They strive always to return the planet to balance regardless of our actions. The flower essences I have created with Nature are all healing patterns that have been freely given to us simply because I asked for it. Such is the sacredness of every plant.

Why do these sacred plants give so much to us? Do they have such love for us that they so grace our lives? To us humans, such receptivity may feel like love. But it's simply the plants fulfilling their job description. Nature intelligence as a whole has the job of maintaining balance, and each plant has its own particular job to do as its part of the whole system. As our planet is shifting energetically, all of nature is changing to accommodate the shift and maintain balance. As nature changes, new plants are appearing, and old plants are receiving new job descriptions. Every plant, and every job it has been tasked with doing, is needed during this intense time of shift. They all are doing their sacred work of maintaining balance. My gratitude goes out to each of them.

To Leave Something of Myself:
Journal Entry, April 17, 2012

Blue on blue. Lighter and darker striations of blue on each petal of each lovely blossom of the hyacinth flower. Each blossom of six radiating petals forms a vortex leading to the inner sanctum where stamens hold their pollen uplifted, waiting for a passing bee. The bee will partake of the enlivening nectar and carry pollen away in pouches on her hind legs. More pollen will cling to her body, only to rub off later as the bee visits other flowers.

The bee is a vital link in the life cycle of the hyacinth flower. Once the bee returns to the hive, she will regurgitate the nectar into a sister worker bee whose job it is to receive nectar and place it into wax cells for the creation of honey. The pollen also will be stored. All summer the worker bees will gather nectar and pollen from those plants that are in bloom. The bees must gather enough nectar and pollen to make enough honey to sustain them over the long winter. Bees can't work when it rains or when the temperature falls below 50 degrees Fahrenheit.

The life of the individual bee is not a weighty matter in the group mind of the hive. The individual bee works so hard in spring or summer, that her life is a mere six weeks long. During that time she will rotate jobs with her sisters. They take turns exploring the vicinity of the hive for new food sources, gathering nectar and pollen, raising brood, and guarding the hive. She does all this work so that the hive may continue once she is gone. The male bees, called *drones,* are not involved in these activities.

The factory that is the hyacinth is not any less busy than the factory that is the hive. Since a seedling, the hyacinth has been growing through its interaction with the elements around it. It's taken in minerals from the soil and water, elements from the air, and sunlight to build itself from seed to plant. The lovely blossoms of the flower are the fullest peak expression of the life force of the hyacinth. The hyacinth also has done all this work so that the next generation of hyacinths may grow and flourish.

So I, too, would like to leave something of myself to benefit those that follow me. I was touched last night when my son Dickon told me that he sees much good in himself that has come from my influence. To consider that some of his goodness has been awakened in him through me is a gift. To believe that I deserve that gift opens a door within me to see my own goodness and acknowledge my own beauty.

The Ways and Means of Healing Plants: Journal Entry, May 2, 2012

Frankincense, Roman chamomile, *Helichrysum italicum*, and ylang ylang—I have created a prescription based on these four essential oils. I uncap the vial of frankincense and thump out the required number of drops into a plastic squeeze bottle. Then I bring the bottle near my nose and whiff the scent into my nostrils. I know that this action excites the olfactory nerves, which carry the information directly to the amygdalae, the seats of our ancient brain. From there, the beneficial effect of the oil reaches the higher brain and the autonomic nervous system.

I re-cap the frankincense, and continue uncapping and thumping out drops from the vials of Roman chamomile, *Helichrysum*, and ylang ylang. Then I fill the remainder of the bottle with almond oil. I cap the bottle, and then shake it to mix the solution evenly together.

Finally, I uncap and take one last sniff to test the effect of all the oils mixed together. Sometimes my prescriptions smell medicinal in a good way, as if to say, "I'm a serious medicine, not some lightweight perfume, and I will seriously heal what ails you with my righteous scent."

Today's prescription smells heavenly, and I think that anyone who smells it will want to have some on hand just for the joy of having it around.

Just the Next Step

Nature mostly just shows me the next step in the process I'm engaged in, and I have to take the rest on faith.

For example, how would I know which flowers to grow or wild harvest to make flower essences? It seemed that my Nature team wanted me to make essences of corn lily (*Veratrum californicum*), tree peony, and quaking aspen, but how did I really know? With the corn lily, I wasn't sure that I could even find it. It was late in the season, too late to find this plant growing at a lower elevation.

I expected to have to look for it higher, near the summit of a mountain where I knew it grew. I had to take it on faith that this next step would answer my questions. On September 3, the Saturday of Labor Day weekend, I packed up all the essence-making supplies I would need and put enough food for a couple of days into our small RV. Skidmore, Skip, and I then took off to look for corn lilies.

First we went to an area where it was known to grow, as referenced by one of my wildflower guides. We found the corn lilies easily, but they were dead. They'd been dried up by the summer heat.

My husband fell into conversation with a man who turned out to be a scientist studying butterflies. I asked him if he knew anywhere that the corn lilies were flourishing. He gave us exact directions to the most amazing corn lilies, vibrant with life and growing tall above our heads along a stream and against the backdrop of craggy Castle Peak. The stream wound through a meadow where a clump of snow was still melting. The next day, in this meadow, near the stream and under the view of the imposing peak, I gathered one of the giant corn lily flowers.

Back at our campsite, I was guided to set up my essence-making bowl on a bamboo board directly on the ground, leveling the board with some rocks. As I set it up, the board was shaded by pine trees. I questioned this inside myself, because I knew I would need three hours of full sun to make the essence. However, I realized that meeting the scientist had not been an accident and that I would never have found these lilies without his help. Or if I had found some lilies in a different area, they might not have been at the peak of perfection as they were here. So I reminded myself not to question the help I was getting now.

I finished setting up the bowl, covering it with one layer of cheesecloth because there were so many insects around. The bowl was still shaded by tall pines, so I sat on a nearby stump and waited. After five minutes, the movement of the sun unexpectedly caused the bowl to be in full sunlight, and it remained so throughout the entire three hours. I then poured the essence into four jars and stabilized them with crystals and the genesa crystal, one jar at a time for one hour each.

With the corn lily, I had stepped out on faith, packed up everything and made all the arrangements as if I were going to find the flower, and serendipitously, a stranger had showed up and pointed the way for me.

With the tree peonies, I had to give up, at least for the moment. I either didn't need them or the time was not right. I tried various avenues to find them, but each attempt led me to a dead end. The connections I had sent out didn't connect. I couldn't force the energy; I had to let it come to me. Maybe events had arranged themselves in such a way that the tree peony was no longer needed. Maybe some other essence or combination of essences would do just as well or better.

With the quaking aspen, I was clearly led to visit a particular stand of them in the Green Creek Wildlife area in

March 2012. The place was covered with snow at the time and it was clearly too soon to make an essence. I was aware that my visit was for the purpose of creating a bond that would bring me back to the location at the right time.

I didn't know when the right time would be. I wanted to collect the female catkins, not the male. And I knew that the male catkins would appear on the trees and broadcast their pollen first. The females would follow a few weeks later. The interval between the arrival of the male and female catkins is why the aspen here reproduce by cloning through their root systems, and not by pollination.

I didn't know when the female catkins would be ready. I tried calling the park rangers and searching for the information in other ways, but to no avail.

In early June, I felt that I could wait no longer. If I didn't go back to the quaking aspen, I would miss them. So I again packed up everything needed and traveled with my husband and dog to the Green Creek Wildlife area, almost a day's journey away from our home.

It turned out that we arrived at just the right time. The day I made the essence was one day before the Venus transit of the Sun. It was a day of high winds, but good sun. The aspen were enthusiastic about the essence making, especially the younger trees. As I picked their catkins, they seemed to be calling to me, "Pick me, pick me."

Later, just as I was bottling the essence, heavy clouds came, obscuring the sun. I received an inner suggestion that I set up the stabilization process in the driver's seat of the RV, instead of outside. About 20 minutes before the end of the stabilization period, it started to hail. We had been planning to spend the night, but as soon as the stabilization was complete, we quickly packed up and drove home so that we would not be stuck in the snow.

DARK NIGHT OF THE SOUL

Now that I've told you about the wonderful and sometimes amazing occurrences that happened to me through living a partnering-with-nature lifestyle, you may think that it's a lifestyle that always fills your life with sweetness and light. But now I entered a phase I call *the dark night of the soul.* The feeling of stuckness became pervasive, tinting my days with shades of gray. I struggled to remain positive, but I couldn't shake the feeling that I was not progressing with my writing because I was not trying hard enough. Or maybe I didn't have the necessary ability or self-development to succeed.

Since I couldn't progress with writing, I told myself to move forward in other areas, but I found it difficult to focus elsewhere. I would begin to chastise myself for procrastinating and wasting time, then I would stop and tell myself that this was probably just a difficult period that I had to go through and that all would be well in the end. Only when I was making flower essences did the gray oppressive feeling lift, and I could perceive myself as a vehicle for the transmission of light.

INDEPENDENCE DAY, JULY 4, 2012:
THE DAY THE DISCOVERY OF THE HIGGS BOSON
PARTICLE IS ANNOUNCED

I make two essences, common mullein (*Verbascum thapsus*) and love-in-a-mist (*Nigella damascena*).

First I gather mullein blossoms, removing the stamens. I connect to the usual Nature team members, except that I forget to connect to the Deva of Mullein. As I usually do,

I ask the plants if they are willing to give blossoms for the making of an essence. There's no difficulty, the six plants in front of me are willing. It's taking a long time because I don't want to touch the blossoms and the stamens are difficult to remove.

After collecting for about an hour, I think I have enough blossoms, but I'm not sure. I ask my team how many more are needed. Still I can't get a clear answer. I get a no answer to, "More than five," and to, "Five," and to, "Less than five." I tell the team I really need their help on this, but still get inconsistent answers. So I sit on the porch for a while, drink some water, and wait. I'm frustrated, but I feel there is an answer that I can find somehow.

After a time, I approach the plants again. Having realized I have forgotten to connect to the deva of the plant, I do that now. Then I ask the plants if they want to give me any additional blossoms for the essence.

As soon as I ask, certain blossoms seem to "light up" or to call out to me. I pick five or six of these, and then no more seem to call out. I ask if that is all the blossoms the plants want to give, and I get a yes. So I use those in addition to the ones I had already picked for the essence.

I have a great many love-in-a-mist flowers, maybe a couple hundred, of all different colors: white, fuchsia, light blue, and dark blue. Still connected to the same team members, I connect to the Deva of *Nigella damascena.* I ask if the flowers are willing to be used for an essence for the healing of humans. I almost always get a yes to this question, but this time, surprisingly, I get a no. It is similar to my experience with the brittlebush the previous spring, except that the *Nigella* doesn't seem as resentful as the brittlebush did. Perhaps that's because I had grown the *Nigella* plants from seed and cared for them, whereas I had wild harvested the brittlebush from right outside Joshua Tree National Park.

I ask if any flowers at all are willing, and I get a yes. So I ask each grouping or section of them if there are any willing within that group. If I get a yes, then I ask each flower until I locate the willing one. In the end, I was able to gather four blossoms, three light blue ones and one fuchsia one. This is enough to make the essence, so I'm satisfied and thank them.

FROM THE PWN HANDBOOK

To me, magic is science that we don't understand yet. The alchemy of homeopathy and the alchemy of flower essences are two magical sciences that have been given to me for my special study and consideration. I have no desire to study these two healing arts using the techniques of conventional science. I'm convinced that the active principles of these medicines cannot be found through the controlled double-blind tests that conventional science loves and demands. Instead I study them through special techniques of attention and listening. And I study them through my connection to the world's greatest authority on how things work: through my connection to Nature.

When I say Nature, please don't think trees and flowers. Think form and organization. Our souls are human, but the form of the body that is the vehicle for the soul is a creation of Nature. Everything we experience through our senses is Nature.

Nature left to itself will always create in balance. Nature doesn't have free will; it has no choice other than to create in balance. We humans have free will, so we can take the building blocks Nature has created—building blocks like carbon, oxygen, and hydrogen—and make unbalanced things with it, such as plastic garbage bags that don't decompose. This free will of ours is a great gift, and a defining characteristic of what it means to be human. But we need Nature's expertise in balance to guide our free will so we can continue to evolve without obliterating ourselves.

I've told you all this about Nature so that you may understand who it is that I'm connecting with when I study homeopathic medicines and flower essences. The source of each of these medicines is a physical substance found in nature: a plant, animal, or mineral that is a substance in form. The homeopathic remedy created from the substance is also in form, but not form as we often understand it. It's not physical in the sense we typically think of, because most of us can't perceive it with our senses. All we perceive is the water or lactose pellets that are the carrier for the medicine.

So if a medicine is in form, but we can't see it, what kind of form is it in? It's in the form of energy, a type of encapsulated healing pattern that is held within water or a sugar pellet carrier, which is released to people, animals, or plants when it's given to them as medicine. If the medicine releases an energy that the recipient can use, a healing response is evoked. Otherwise the plant, animal, or person will just ignore the extraneous energy and it will not affect them. There are no side effects with such medicines.

How is the original substance—the plant, animal, or mineral used to make the medicine—or more precisely, the healing pattern gathered from it, made into medicine? In the case of a homeopathic remedy, the substance is diluted and shaken serially. We dilute, then shake, and dilute and shake again until there's often nothing of the original substance left—only its energetic healing pattern. In the case of a flower essence, the petals of the flower are floated on water in the sun for about three hours, releasing the healing pattern into the water.

I'm continually learning more about these medicines and expanding my understanding. I can tell you that my continuing education in Nature's curriculum is mostly experiential, and that Nature clearly wants me to learn by doing. As I learn, I'm using what I'm learning. In my garden, with my clients, in my writing, and down to the core of who I am and what I'm being in this lifetime.

WAITING FOR CLARITY: JOURNAL ENTRY, SEPTEMBER 21, 2012

There's something not right about the concept for the book I want to write. Somehow it needs to be more anecdotal and less neatly laid out. I would rather not be thinking, *I really should be writing today.* I'd rather just be writing or not writing because that is what is flowing out of me (or not) by just being myself.

The other night, I spoke to about 60 people about GMOs. Why did I volunteer to do that? Not because I thought, *I really should be speaking more, so I'll volunteer.* I spoke because it was a job that needed to be done, and I knew I could do it and do it well. That's why I volunteered. People asked me beforehand if I was nervous about speaking in front of a group, and I said no. I really wasn't. I knew what I wanted to say, I knew I could say it clearly and satisfactorily, so I just did it.

It seems to me that the projects I'm actively working on are ones that need to be done, and I know how to do them well. So I'm doing them. The activist work on GMO labeling is like that for me. I feel confident that the work needs to be done by someone, and somehow my number got called and I stepped up. I never question it, it just feels right.

The GMO work doesn't really stretch me. I already know how to facilitate meetings, create websites and email lists, and lead people in action in this way. I'm well trained and well practiced.

The work I did recently on my son's website and accounting system was a bit different. I had to learn the QuickBooks software for the accounting system and greatly expand my knowledge of WordPress software to set up the website. But even learning new software isn't that much of a stretch. I have lots of experience in learning new software; I know how to do that.

The projects I'm not working on are the flower essences and the book. When working on either of these, I feel as if I'm walking off the edge of a cliff into thin air, and trusting that the air will support me and that I won't fall and land on my face. That used to be okay with me. I had to summon my courage, yes, but I was able to do it and I did actually move forward on those projects.

What changed? One thing that changed with the flower essences is that I got blocked in setting up some aspects of the business. Although I had been blocked before with the flower essences, especially when the creating the label, I had just chipped away at the problem for months and finally resolved it. This time, I didn't chip away; I stopped working on the essence project altogether.

I told myself that it was appropriate to do so while I worked on the GMO labeling and on my son's business—and maybe that was correct, maybe that really was the reason and not an excuse—and I'm clearly in a much better position to create the flower essence website now that I know how to use WordPress.

What changed about the book is somewhat deeper and murkier to my understanding. Let's see if I can set forward some of the factors that have impacted my writing; and if in doing so, things get clearer.

When I started writing this book, I quickly found out that my original idea of how the book was to be written was wrong. I had thought that my team of supporting entities would essentially dictate the book to me and I would write down what they were saying.

I don't usually hear exact words; I receive pictures and concepts and have to translate them into words assisted by a lot of questions. I'm constantly asking, "Is this wording right?" So my original idea of taking dictation was challenging enough, and then it turned out that the entities wanted me to write the book myself, from my own knowledge.

It appears that the most important outcome of the book is to be my personal growth. The benefits for the reader apparently need to be secondary, at least from my vantage point.

I started writing the parts of the book that I could best write from my own knowledge, even though I was still hoping to get some level of assistance from the entities. But it got harder and harder to receive assistance from them. And I don't know if that's because they wanted me to write the book without their assistance or because I couldn't hear them clearly or for some other unknown reason.

Eventually, I got to a chapter in the book that I couldn't

write entirely from my own knowledge. In the absence of dictation, I got stuck and stopped writing until I could get clarity on my next steps.

Today I'm still waiting, hoping for clarity. I feel as though I have piles of scrap cloth that are destined to be put together to create a quilt and I just can't see the pattern or how to create what is yet to be.

QUANDARIES: JOURNAL ENTRY, OCTOBER 8, 2012, SHAMANIC VALLEY CAMPGROUND

In the summer of 1978, Machaelle Small Wright's team told her to plant and harvest, and to do nothing else in the garden that year. To help her do this, Nature kept her occupied by assigning her the task of building a Sioux tipi from a kit that required her to cut and sand the poles and sew together yards of canvas. This tipi had a real purpose in their work, but it also occupied her time, making it easier for her to stay out of the garden.

This summer, my vegetable garden didn't flourish. I was led not to plant much and what I did grow looked malnourished and depleted, even though I had used fertilizer. Actually the cover crop from the winter before had also not done well, which I attributed to the use of seeds with self-activating inoculant that apparently didn't activate. Very little of the cover crop sprouted and grew, which could be why the summer garden plants looked weak and produced so few vegetables.

I didn't spend much time in the garden. Much of the time I was unable to work there because I had injured my left knee and was unable to kneel on the ground. All work was done stooping over, and I could only do it for a short time without hurting my back. Also, I just felt unmotivated to garden.

I've been spending more time following U.S. politics in general, as well as global news. I'm especially looking for information related to how the ascension of the planet is affecting political systems around the world. The global stories that I'm most closely following are known as the "European Debt Crisis" and the shifts in the Arab world following the "Arab Spring."

I see these as hopeful signs. The European monetary crisis is hopeful because it points to an overreach by those controlling the global economy. People have come to the limit of their ability to produce wealth for those controllers and cannot be forced by further oppression into doing so.

The Arab crisis reflects the global desire of people everywhere for greater justice and equality. This desire is an integral part of the dynamic of our planet's ascension process and therefore cannot be suppressed. It will continue to surface in the demands of people throughout the world.

I'm not sure about the usefulness of my desire to follow these events so closely. The process appears to be unfolding regardless of my attention, so it's possibly a waste of time for me to track it so thoroughly. It should be enough for me to know that it's happening, and that I only need to focus on my particular role in world events.

Actually, what is my role? I'm not a world leader. I have taken some limited local roles. I organized and facilitated two local forums on the Affordable Care Act before it became law and lately I've coordinated action supporting the labeling of GMOs. I'm a progressive, but only talk politics with close friends. I don't attempt to persuade others. Other than these local actions and casting my vote, do I have a role?

Possibly my team is using my interest in politics to keep

me occupied just as they used Machaelle Small Wright's tipi to keep her out of her garden. That would explain why I feel as though I'm waiting for something. I would like the time for greater action to be now, but my will power that wants action doesn't seem to connect with any project or activity that's genuine. If I try to work on my writing, my garden, or my flower essences, I feel as though I'm faking it. I don't know if it would be best for me to work on these anyway on the theory that I need to "fake it until I make it" or if it would be best to wait until soul-level desire impels me forward.

The one project I'm working on that is clearly proceeding from soul-level choice is my work on the labeling of GMOs. A genetically modified plant is produced by bombarding the DNA of one species with DNA from another species. Often a food plant, such as corn, is crossed with DNA from a microbe. These two species would never genetically combine across the species barrier in nature.

There are studies that indicate that genetically modified foods may be affecting the climbing rates of diabetes, heart disease, autism, and other diseases. For example, when corn is crossed with DNA from *Bacillus thuringiensis* bacteria, which is toxic to some insects, the resulting corn is toxic to insects in the field. Studies indicate that the corn may also be toxic to humans, possibly causing leaky gut and other intestinal diseases.

GMOs are an attempt by humans to alter the archetype of different organisms—often food crops—without the cooperation of Nature. The archetype of each plant was created by Nature and brought into manifestation on our planet in order to fulfill the needs and desires of the planet and those incarnated here. Because a GMO food has been altered without the cooperation of Nature, it cannot contain the vitality of conventional food. This is why I'm passionate about the GMO work.

I know that I'm positioned to take actions on my local level that are needful to be taken and that I can do them well. I have the right skill set and the time to do them. The required actions seem to flow from me naturally. They are work. I need to apply commitment, focus, intelligence, and effort. But I don't question if I should do them. I also don't question if I've done enough. I do what I know needs to be done in the moment, and then I stop. I sleep well at night and don't worry if I should have done more.

I am certain that nothing can ultimately deny the force within me toward soul evolution. How I am to evolve, the steps I am to go through, and the experiences I need to have will ultimately take place, whether in this lifetime or in some other. But I also have the desire to complete the mission I accepted for this lifetime. I don't want to miss an opportunity to grow due to lack of diligence. And I'd like to contribute what I can to the ongoing evolution of the planet in this unique time. I'm sure that is why I was born into this life. I don't want to miss any opportunities to play a part in grounding the new dynamic fully into the planet.

I realize that the feeling of "not doing enough" is not helpful to me or to others. And I realize that I can't use will power to force myself to do more work. Any work done from that mind frame would lack the qualities needed for success. So I suppose my only realistic option is to trust myself and my soul's direction and purpose, and that all will transpire for my greater good in its own time.

In the meantime, I'd like to use this quieter time to become more skilled at distinguishing which thoughts and messages are coming from my higher self and which are coming from the world around me and being assimilated as my own. I sense that my desire to piece together a congruent picture of how the world works leads me to accept information that is either untrue or irrelevant to my concerns. This causes unnecessary strain and diversion. Information that I really need comes to hand easily. For example, there is no strain for me in understanding the relationship between plant archetypes and GMOs.

Instead of finding answers from the outside, let me listen clearly to the promptings from the inside, and follow those wherever they lead with passion and diligence.

My True Home: Journal Entry, October 9, 2012, Shamanic Valley Campground (A Day after Writing the Preceding Entry)

One day, within a scintilla of time, almost from one moment to the next, my long dark night of the soul ends. A sentence in a book releases a fountain of sorrow within me. It refers to the difficulty of operating from one framework while living in another.

My inner response is, *Yes, what about that?* and then I burst into tears. I am relating the sentence I've read to my seeming isolation here on Earth. I'm operating from one framework, the eternal life of my soul, while living in another, my temporal earthly life. I quickly reach for my computer and write the following words.

> *I feel alone and abandoned here, even though I know that I'm protected and surrounded with love at all times. But it's a knowing, not a feeling. I need to feel it embracing*

me, strengthening me, and supporting me continuously. I need the love and support of my true home and family to infuse the air I breathe and to be woven into the fabric of life as I experience it. And somehow I think that the reason I can't feel all this is because of some lack in myself. I know the love and support has to be there, I just don't have the ability to discern it. It's my fault, because if only I knew how to look, I would see it everywhere.

I'm still crying. From somewhere deep inside me, resolution breaks through my stuckness. I refuse to accept the aloneness. I demand to live from the reality that am always being loved and minded—every second, with every breath. Right here, right now, as I continue to type the words, I take my stand.

This is the step that I am now taking, to perceive the love and support that I have as it enfolds and supports me in every moment of my life. I acknowledge that love and support from my family are my constant companions, and that my connection to my true home is unbroken. I am never alone. My family is with me always, loving and supporting me. I can lean on them, accepting nurturing. This gives me strength and endurance for whatever tasks come my way.

With new resolve, after writing this journal entry, my doubt and isolation vanish. My darkness lifted, I return home to find myself unblocked. With new clarity, I begin writing a different book—this book—with a different purpose, which is to show how my relationship with Nature has transformed my life.

CHAPTER 9

THE LAST MIMZY

Early in 2013, I received a message that Ursa was making arrangements for another Mimzy event to take place in April. She explained that this event would complete the Mimzy Project that began near Mount Shasta in April 2009. At that time, she heard the voices of beings who asked her to return in a year bringing at least 12 others with her. As I related in Chapter 2, I was one of the participants in this Mimzy event. I now began to consider whether I was also being called to participate in the 2013 event.

I phoned Sky, who said she was planning to fly to California from the East Coast in order to participate. I couldn't pass up a chance to be on Mount Shasta with Sky again! That did it. I made arrangements to attend, and Sky and I agreed to room together.

Later Kalia said that she was also flying in from the East Coast. Now I was doubly glad I had decided to attend! Kalia also invited me to attend a three-day crystal bowl class to be taught by Bev Wilson, proprietor of the Crystal Room in the City of Mount Shasta.

201

FIRST CRYSTAL BOWL SESSION, APRIL 1, 2013

There are four of us in the class: Tess, Marcia, Kalia, and myself. All of us were in the 2010 Mimzy Project event and we're happy to be together again.

We meet in a special room in the Crystal Room store that Bev has created to house crystal singing bowls that are not for sale. This is the room she uses for teaching about the bowls.

Bev tells us that the crystal bowls are conscious entities that can teach us through her. They channel teachings to us from spirit. Since the bowls are conscious, a connection with a bowl is a relationship, and will be unique for each person.

Bev encourages us to learn through direct experience with the bowls. She tells us not to take notes during the class, but to focus on our direct perceptions.

We experience three types of vibration from each crystal bowl: its sound or tone when played, the minerals used in the coating, and the color. The sound is created by tapping or circling the edge of the bowl with a suede mallet. The sound vibrations are not just heard by the ear, but are perceived by the entire body.

Each bowl activates a specific chakra most intensely. For example, the low C bowl activates the root chakra, while the high C bowl activates a chakra above the crown. The other tones and corresponding areas are: low C-sharp Sexual, D Sacral, D-sharp Lower Dan Tien (below the navel), E Solar Plexus, F Heart, F-sharp Thymus, G Throat, G-sharp Zeal point, A Third Eye, A-sharp Pineal, and B Crown. I haven't previously been aware of the Zeal point, which is located near the medulla oblongata at the base of the skull, and is sometimes referred to as the "well of dreams."

All of the crystal singing bowls are made with quartz crystal. Some of the bowls also have minerals or gems added such as gold, silver, titanium, platinum, amethyst, citrine, moldavite, and ruby. In addition to the tone, we are also affected by the vibration of the crystal and any minerals contained in the bowl, in the same way that a crystal or stone in our environment has a vibratory effect on us.

In addition to classic white-frosted bowls, there are also clear bowls and bowls of many different colors. While the tone affects the physical body, the minerals and color affect the subtle body. The subtle impact is received a moment later in time, after the physical impact.

Bev introduces us to one of her bowls that functions as bio-feedback loop. We learn that if you play the bowl when you are solidly grounded and present in the moment, the bowl produces a deep tone. If you play the same bowl when not solidly grounded, it produces a high tone, and the high tone will tend to unground you further, making you feel spacey. As you play the bowl, you can sense what you are doing with your energy to cause the tone to be low or high. As you do more of what creates the low tone, you become more solidly grounded in yourself.

EARLY MORNING LEY LINE WORK, APRIL 2, 2013

That evening, the four of us have dinner with Zara. Tess, Marcia, me, and Kalia had met her during the 2010 Mimzy event, and we all enjoy the chance to reconnect again. That night Kalia and I stay at in an apartment above the Crystal Room, bathing in the intense crystalline energy. In the morning, we meet with Zara again for breakfast. Afterwards Zara takes us to the fish hatchery area. She explains to us that ley line energy comes down from the mountain and passes through the area. She positions us on ley lines above an underground stream. Once positioned, we chant some of the 72 names of God, an auspicious start for our day. Then, bidding goodbye to Zara, we head back to the Crystal Room for our next class.

SECOND CRYSTAL BOWL SESSION, APRIL 2, 2013

Bev tells us that broken, cracked, or chipped bowls can sometimes be mended, but only if the bowl chooses to be mended. If they so choose, they may be stronger for their challenging experience and will express a greater depth of character and compassion. I call one of her mended bowls the wabi-sabi bowl since it is perfect because of its imperfection. I have an intense experience of connection while playing this bowl, which produces a slow low tone suffused with compassion.

Another intense experience for me is to hold one called "the elemental bowl." It's a practitioner bowl, meaning that it is formed with a long rod or handle on what would otherwise be the bottom of the bowl, and you set the bowl down on the rim. The handle allows a practitioner to easily hold the bowl while working with a client. The elemental bowl is decorated with images of fairies, flowers, and butterflies painted and fused into the outer surface coating. Bev explains that she keeps it in the classroom to please the elementals, and that it doesn't want to be played.

I connect with the bowl through my heart and feel a wave of love and appreciation flowing over me and out to the bowl. Tears spill from my eyes as I begin to show the bowl my place. In my imagination, I show the bowl the vortex on Skidmore and my land, our chickens and bees, the place I make flower essences, and the place I stabilize them. The bowl shows me that the red Venus flower with thick black stamens is coming closer into manifestation, as if it is almost within my reach. It also shows me a concept for the packaging of essential oil and flower essence roll-ons. In this visualization, I see an image of six to eight roll-on vials in a box similar to a child's crayon box with the vials in a row like the fat crayons of preschoolers.

The bowl also shows me a type of roller top for the vials that can be interchanged with a spray top. That way, the same vial can function as either a roll-on or a spray. I've never seen such an interchangeable cap, so it may be a device that hasn't been invented yet.

After this experience, Bev tells me that the bowls want me to know that they appreciate my work with the elementals. Since I hadn't mentioned my work with Nature, I feel stunned and gratified that they can see me so clearly.

Later, at 8:30 that evening, Bev and the bowls do a crystal bowl activation for us while we lie down and allow the sound to wash over us. The activation itself is beyond words and I sleep soundly afterwards.

THIRD CRYSTAL BOWL SESSION, APRIL 3, 2013

Bev begins by explaining the strategy the bowls chose for the previous evening's activation. The first part of the activation was to open, clear, and balance us. They addressed each of our chakras in turn with both tone and color. In the second part, the chakras were integrated and space opened for expansion. Finally, the expansion was integrated and stabilized. The entire activation took maybe an hour, although I couldn't estimate it well because such an activation seems timeless.

Today we have each chosen a bowl from the showroom

to work with—or more accurately, a bowl has chosen us. Two bowls chose Kalia, so she brings both of them into the classroom. I have been chosen by one made with an alchemical coating called *lepidolite* that contains the element lithium. The coating has been unevenly applied deliberately, creating dark streaks that give the bowl a wild look. The streaks look like black raven's feathers against the dark blue of the bowl.

When I play the bowl, it has a high tone, which surprises me because the other C bowls have a low tone and are associated with the root chakra. This bowl is also much smaller than the other C bowls. Bev explains that this is a high C associated with a chakra above the crown—it's an octave higher than the others.

At first I can't make the bowl play very loudly. Bev encourages me to connect with it through my heart. After a time, I come to understand that we are working together like a rider and a horse, and I start to coax it. Finally I say, "Giddy-up," and it goes, playing loudly and strongly. Bev calls it "barely tame" in reference to its wildness.

I love it. In my mind, I show it pictures of our place, of Skidmore and Skip, of the chickens and bees, vortex, flower essences, genesa, and my office. I tell it I'm not a good housekeeper and if it lived with us, it might get a bit dusty at times. But I ask if it would like to be with us anyhow, and I sense that it is willing though not determined either way.

When the class is over, we part from Bev knowing that we will see her again with the entire Mimzy group in three days. My respect for her and her knowledge is unbounded.

MIMZY GATHERING APRIL 3, 2013

We gather in joy for the 2013 Mimzy event. We are all

staying together in the same motel. Everyone seems to arrive within minutes of each other, so we all mill around the parking lot, hugging each other and exchanging joyous greetings. So many friendships from the 2010 event are rekindled. There are new participants to meet and enjoy. We are 22 people connected in a field of intention.

Later that evening, during our first meal together, Kalia beckons me to come outside. The others follow me out onto a balcony and Kalia points out clouds around Mount Shasta that appear to be cloaking spaceships.

After dinner and sharing, most of our group goes to Bunny Flat, the cross country ski area on Mount Shasta that is the highest part of the mountain you can drive to in the winter. I had gone to Bunny Flat with Marcia and Tess the afternoon before, so I stay at the motel to call Skidmore and write in my journal.

Here is Sky's description of her time on the mountain that night:

> *We went up to Bunny Flat. It was dark, but you could see the mountain. We were meandering around. I walked up the path, but my foot sunk into the snow, so I turned around. Kalia was behind me saying, "Can you see the beings of light?" She was saying it for people who don't see.*
>
> *Then I saw pillars of light coming down, and many other people who couldn't see them before, could see them then. You could see the energy around the trees, could see their light. I looked into sky. It was overcast, but I could see a couple of stars. One star started to morph into an oval shape, a white light, not big, the same size as a star.*

It was expanding and contracting, and then it started spiraling. It had a pinkish color on the end of it.

For me who doesn't see, it was gratifying that I saw this now. Other people were able to see things, too. My biggest vision was the pillars of light and this star.

Kalia came up to me and asked if I knew how to chant, "Kadoish, Kadoish, Kadoish, Adonai Tsebayoth." That's music to God's ears; we chanted it for quite a while.

That chant was one of the chants we had done the day before with Zara, one of her favorites.

Even though I missed seeing the streaming pillars of light, I'm glad I stayed behind because it was the only time during the entire trip that I was able to actually talk to Skidmore, rather than just leaving a message. He told me to buy the lepidolite crystal bowl if I really wanted it, even though it was expensive. I was so happy to receive this expression of his love and support.

RETURN TO THE WATER SITES, APRIL 4, 2013

The next day the entire Mimzy group visits the four water sites where we performed ceremony and set crystals three years before.

I am one of the drivers, with Kalia, Claire, Sybil, and Sky as my passengers. Kalia will be leading a ceremony at each site, beginning with the headwaters of the Sacramento River. In the car on the way to the headwaters, Kalia asks the four of us to form a star around the spring, so each of us is fairly equidistant from the others and we form a semi-circle around the spring. The other participants will hold points between us. We'd like to form a complete circle as we did three years before, but we're not sure that new landscaping will allow that.

Later I find out that one of our group, Sage, has been guided to hold a position on the other side of the river, beyond some trees to Kalia's left, completing a circle. My position is to be to Kalia's right.

At the headwaters, we begin our ceremony with smudging, ceremoniously clearing each person's aura with smoke from burning sage. There is a light rain, making it hard to keep the sage burning. The flowing water, the wind, and the rain are so loud that we can't hear each other well. My assignment is to approach each person who has been smudged and tell them, "We are encircling the spring. Find the spot that's right for you." Once all are smudged and in place, Kalia begins the ceremony.

As Kalia calls in the directions, one of our group, Gareth, comes to each person and asks them to tone. I begin toning, "Om." As I do, I go energetically into the ground beneath the spring. I become aware of the Lemurian temple that exists on a higher dimension at these headwaters. It is now much lower in elevation than three years ago; so low it is almost touching the ground. As I pull it energetically toward me, it grounds itself further and embeds itself into the soil with what feels like a click. Perhaps I am actually grounding it, or maybe I am now seeing it from a timeless perspective as the grounded structure it is.

Later I learn that Sybil has had a similar experience of the descent of the temple. She saw it descending as if in an elevator shaft into the center of the Earth. In her vision, it can descend further later, but it is now at the level of our ground. The similarity of our two experiences lets me know that what we have been dreaming and longing for—the grounding of a higher consciousness on earth—is now here.

BIRD HEAVEN

Our second stop is Lower Klamath Falls National Wildlife Refuge, or as we call it, Bird Heaven. We gather for ceremony on the same observation platform we used three years before.

On this day, as in April 2010, there is plenty of water and numerous birds are present. The energetic temple atop the platform feels activated, not old and abandoned as it felt when Sky and I visited it in September 2010. At that time, the sluices were closed and there was no water and few birds. We had reactivated it with soil balancing and Sky's crystal bowl playing. Either our reactivation held or the presence of water caused it to activate.

Before the ceremony, I offer small crystals to anyone who wants them. Many take them and toss them into the water at the end of the ceremony.

During the ceremony, I feel very calm, as though the ceremony isn't anything to be excited about because bringing that energy in is like breathing. There is nothing to try for.

Later, as we leave Bird Heaven, I see a huge flock of snow geese rising up like a cloud some distance ahead of us. There are also birds lined up along the edge of the road as if standing sentinel. Kalia and I interpret both formations of birds as an expression of gratitude for the work we have done.

LAKE SHASTINA

Our third stop is Lake Shastina. We go first to a picnic area to eat the lunches we have brought. As I finish eating, Sky comes up to me and says she is not feeling well. She feels ungrounded, as though her energy is not in her body. I put my arms around her torso and send grounding energy to her body, but to no avail. Sky moves away to sit on a nearby log, and I go to find Kalia and ask for her help.

Later, Sky explains:

> *When I do this work, I always connect to the earth, but I really want to go up. This time I went up and I was out of my body. When we stopped for lunch, I was in an altered state. I went up so far, I couldn't come right back in.*
>
> *When Kalia was working on grounding me, part of me didn't want to come back. She was putting out quite a lot of energy to bring me back, but it wasn't working. I said, "There's a part of me that doesn't want to come back," and she said, "You need to talk to that part of yourself."*
>
> *Later, during the ceremony, when Kalia was drumming, I sat on a rock and I could feel the beings surrounding me. Finally I felt my root chakra open up, and I was back. But it took a long time.*

After lunch we drive as close as we can to the dam and hike the rest of the way, almost to the dam. Kalia selects a clearing that is protected from the brisk wind for our ceremony. Kalia and another group member, Vanessa, use large, round, Native American-style handheld drums to envelop each person in sound by drumming on both sides of them. Kalia says this is to activate the cells of the body.

During the ceremony, I feel a deep calm. My feeling of not needing to strive for anything that I experienced at Bird Heaven persists during the Lake Shastina ceremony as well.

Afterward, we share our experience with the group. Several people speak of dramatic high experiences and perceptions. My sense is simply that we've now arrived. Where we wanted to go three years ago, we're now there. This is the peace and healing that we've been wanting for our planet.

Claire says something similar about peace as well. She didn't experience anything that seemed amazing, but received the even more amazing perception that peace is possible; it's here and we can have it.

As we walk back to the cars, one of the men, Casey, who's from Ireland, sings an Irish song so beautifully that it brings tears to my eyes.

We have one more ceremony to complete our work for the day. On the way to Lake Siskiyou, we see a lovely rainbow to the east. Kalia says that we are being thanked and we should take in and acknowledge the gratitude expressed.

LAKE SISKIYOU

At Lake Siskiyou, we hike to the picnic tables where we'd been three years before. The water line is higher, making the lake look different. We cannot see Mount Shasta because the sky is overcast, but I point out the direction of the mountain for Casey and some of the others who haven't been here before.

During the ceremony, Kalia talks about experiencing the energy body as two intersecting crystalline triangular pyramids, or *tetrahedrons*. One pyramid pointing upward intersects the other, which points down. This forms a *merkaba,* or light body vehicle, which can be used to move from one dimension or level to another.

Near the close of the ceremony, we energetically visit Medicine Lake, including it in our energy grid.

After the ceremony, I return with several others to the parking lot. Some of our group remains at the lake longer, returning more slowly. They see a magnificent light show in the sky as the sun sets.

Later, Sage describes our time at Lake Siskiyou and the setting sun:

> *At Siskiyou, Kalia our earth mother guide led us in ceremony and prayer to Mount Shasta. Casey sang an Irish prayer and Sybil sang an ancient Japanese prayer that was so powerful. Tess sang, and after her song her body was vibrating. Tess reached out and connected with two trees to sustain herself. When she took her hands off the trees, they had become crystalline. They were shimmering, sparkling. Light shimmered across the lake and the clouds in the sky opened up.*
>
> *Those in the know saw portals opening and colors of joy. At one time there was in the sky a blue area surrounded with white, the eye of God acknowledging appreciation of our healing energy. Ursa went into her own world in space and time. She returned to the present world when Airen called out. Ursa's dog absolutely stood guard to protect her. Her stance told us to stay away, as if she knew Ursa was within and gone into another dimension of time and space.*
>
> *Kalia was ecstatic, her body vibrating in awe of what was happening. Around the sun and that whole part of the sky were shimmering colors of opalescent magenta, blue and gold. What I believe were portals were like brilliant white flames, back-lit from the sun like an opening.*

MOUNT SHASTA PYRAMID, APRIL 5, 2013

The next morning, before breakfast, Sky feels that something is trying to arise within her. She feels alone and abandoned by her true tribe. Like Christ in the garden of Gethsemane, she is lamenting, "Why have you forsaken me?"

I receive the intuition to read to her from the manuscript of this book. I read her three paragraphs from the October 9, 2012 entry at the end of Chapter 8, in which I describe feeling alone and abandoned until I gathered my resolution and demanded to live from the reality that I am always being loved and minded. As I read the entry to her, emotionally I begin to re-experience the moment of feeling abandoned and the change to knowing that I am loved, and I begin to weep.

Sky is weeping as well. Later she says that it was necessary that she was able to say, "I need to feel love and connection," before going in the pyramid.

After breakfast, we pack lunches and drive to the Mount Shasta pyramid. It is an overcast day, but decidedly different from the Easter Sunday three years before when we had driven there in a snow storm.

Once we enter the pyramid and sit or lay down, Ursa asks us each to state an intention for whom we are being.

Sky says, "I am the grid of stillness."

I say that I am a partner with Nature.

Kalia says that she is working with water in response to draught.

After each of us has spoken, Ursa has us move to new positions, forming concentric circles and making aisles so that Ariel can do body work on us. Ariel then moves in a circle, working a bit on each person. Meanwhile Ursa plays deeply resonant, large crystal bowls. She tells us each to ground our tailbones energetically into the earth. We continue to do this while Ariel moves in her circle around the pyramid, working on each person.

Later Sage says that Ariel was like the Divine Mother, giving us each love in a magnificent way.

While Ariel is still working on us, I am amazed by a completely unexpected experience. I find myself energetically issuing the order, "Okay, Hyperithon, send in the spaceships." I do not say this out loud. It is clearly not a random thought in my mind, but a personal communication between me and another conscious being. It is also an unexpected communication that I have not consciously chosen to make.

Once I make it, I am stunned. I'm not even aware that I am on speaking terms with Hyperithon, the head of the White Brotherhood Department of Science and Technology. I know from reading Machaelle Small Wright's book *The Mount Shasta Mission* that he is involved in White Brotherhood missions when spaceships are used. It is now clear to me that I have been prepared in my dream work to give Hyperithon the high sign when our group is settled in the pyramid and the time has come for the ships to enter.

I look around the pyramid to see if I can spot any ships entering. We are all lying on our backs, heads aimed toward the center of the pyramid. I look upward with the soft, unfocused gaze that sometimes allows me to see things in another dimension. In the corner of my eye, I see a shadowy shape about a foot tall and two to three feet in length moving diagonally above me from the right toward the center of the pyramid. As soon as I focus on it, I can't see it.

I don't see a spaceship again until much later in the day. There may have been more than one, since I have requested,

"Send in the spaceships," plural. Even when I don't see them, I am aware of their presence, and I sense that they are affecting the consciousness of us all.

One remarkable aspect of this experience is how unremarkable it feels. Although I am stunned that I am clearly taking part in plans that I consciously know nothing about, otherwise the event has an everyday feel about it. Working with the White Brotherhood should feel like an everyday event since I work with them almost every day. But I would have thought that the presence of a spaceship would feel more special and otherworldly than it does, even though the ship I saw was a very small spaceship—or at least appeared small to my vision. It's interesting to me that I feel quite matter-of-fact about it.

If you find this whole spaceship thing a bit too much, believe me, I sympathize. I've tried to faithfully record the events of both this and the 2010 Mimzy event, including the sightings of spaceships on occasion. But I've been a bit leery of the whole thing. Before I went to Shasta, I would sometimes visualize the Mimzy event and what I might end up writing about it. I didn't imagine that I would be saying that I encountered a spaceship. But there it is. If I'm going to record what has happened to the best of my ability, I have to describe it as honestly as I can. Even if you think I'm nuts.

After some time in the pyramid, we leave to eat our lunches. It is overcast and a bit rainy, so I eat in my car with Sky, Kalia, and Casey, the singer of Irish ballads. The weather for the whole Mimzy event has been interesting. It was predicted to rain all the days of the Mimzy event, but the only time it has really rained so far was when we were at the headwaters, and even then it was just a light rain. The rest of the time, we've had beautiful weather when we are outside. One day it was raining when we woke up, but the rain stopped by the time we left the motel. It also rained one evening while we were in a restaurant, but not before or after.

After lunch, it takes a long time to get back into the pyramid because Claire, Shelly, and Darci are working with selenite swords to clear the upper chakras of each person as he or she enters. The sword is held close to the person's body, though not touching it, with the tip pointed at a chakra. The practitioner invokes a stream of light with intention, directing it through the sword, clearing and activating the chakra.

After we get settled, Ursa leads us again to work with the root and sacral chakras, using our diaphragm and chanting to absorb the power of the earth.

At some point, Claire sees the spaceship. She tells the group that it is sitting on a rug which is covering the central part of the floor directly beneath the top point of the pyramid. The rug is woven of strips of cloth forming concentric ovals of different colors. Most of the ovals are of dark colors, but there is one white or light-colored oval that looks to her like the sides of a bathtub. It has the appearance of being raised like an edge rather than flat. The spaceship is inside the light-colored oval.

At this time, I cannot see the spaceship. I say, "Claire, I did call in a spaceship, but I didn't do it on purpose." By which I mean that I didn't do it with conscious intention.

I do see it maybe half an hour later. It is about the same size as the shadowy shape I saw before. It is resting on the center of the rug as Claire described. This time I can look directly at it without it disappearing. It looks like it has either a clear sunroof over the top or it has the top open somehow.

I can see scores or maybe even hundreds of figures looking up at us. Each one appears to be about five inches tall and thin, shaped a bit like a shard of rock. I think these figures are people, but not from our dimension.

Since I called Hyperithon, I reason that they are either White Brotherhood members or beings who are working with the White Brotherhood. I wave to them, but can't tell if they see me or not.

Later Ariel tells me that she also saw a spaceship. She describes it as being about same size and with many passengers of a similar size and shape as the ones I saw. She emphasizes that the most important part of the experience for her was a feeling of intense relatedness to these beings.

Our last ritual in the pyramid is one we come to call the *love baths*. Each person takes a turn standing in the center of the pyramid while the rest of the group tones and showers love on them. The high tip of the pyramid has a clear opening like a small round skylight. When we begin the love baths, the light from this opening is shining on the person below. As the sun is setting, and we continue to do the baths, it grows darker until we can't see who the person in the center is. It eventually becomes so dark that it is difficult to maneuver from our seats to the center without tripping or bumping into something. I am grateful that Sybil, who is sitting close to me, tones out my name during my turn so others can know who is there.

Later Sky tells me that at some point the pyramid seemed to disappear for her. She looked up, and all she saw was stars. She says:

> *I started weeping, because they were from the place*
> *I come from and they were showing me their presence as*

a star. I looked up and said, "Thank you for coming." It was a beautiful moment for me. Just a few hours after I had been crying, "Where are you?" they showed up. In the center, I looked up and saw what I can call the central sun. It was right there with its rays coming out left and right. Wherever that galaxy is, that is my home.

When we leave the pyramid, several of us drive up the mountain to Bunny Flat. I drive with Sky as my only passenger. It is good that I have all-wheel drive, because it is foggy and snowing on the mountain. I drive slowly and carefully and maybe because of this, time seems to slow down and our journey seems pervaded with stillness. After some time on the mountain, we return to the motel, expecting to go snowshoeing the next afternoon.

Mimzy Crystal Bowl Class, April 6, 2013

The next morning, Bev presents a crystal bowl class to our entire Mimzy group. The class covers a portion of the information Bev presented to Kalia, Tess, Marcia, and me in our three-day class.

Before the class begins, Kalia asks me if I would be willing to forgo the group's planned snowshoe hike to Upper Sand Flat in order to go with her, Tess, and Marcia to a cave known as Pluto's Cave. Naturally, I check with my Nature team and get a yes for Pluto's Cave. Kalia asks me to talk to Sky to find out if she also wants to come.

I approach Sky and start to ask her, but only get as far as saying, "Kalia has an alternate adventure planned this afternoon and wants to know if you want to come," when Sky says yes. She tells me that she doesn't need to know where we are going; just knowing that we will be working with Kalia is enough.

Later I ask Sky why she was so sure. She says that something is being transmitted to her through Kalia. She'd like to know who Kalia is to her, what their relationship has been outside of this lifetime. She says, "I'm being educated, though I don't know what about."

I agree with her saying, "Her field organizes my field in a way that's beneficial to both, like a strong magnet lining up all the electrons in the most auspicious way. She's always pointing out things to see or notice. She's always coaxing our perception."

After the bowl class, I ask Bev to help Sky select the right bowl for her to buy. She hasn't planned on buying one; she still has the one that she played when we were in Oregon three years before. But earlier, when I was telling her about Bev and about the bowls, she thought, "I'd like to get one, but I'm not going to." Then she heard a voice saying, "You need to get a bowl from Mount Shasta and from the amazing crystal bowl woman," who she hadn't even met yet.

Now Bev asks her if she knows how to get a yes using kinesiology with her whole body, swaying forward or back. But Sky doesn't use that technique, she just uses her intuition.

Later she explains her process.

I started browsing the bowls and was drawn to the indigo-colored bowls. Normally, I have to play them. I picked the first one up. This bowl was thinner than my old bowl, and I could feel its vibration in my hands. Something told me that it was not the one. Below it was one with the same structure. I picked it up and looked into it. I saw four dots, and when I see the number 4 that is always a sign. I knew immediately it was the bowl. I didn't even have to play it at that point. Then Bev told me, "These four dots are Egyptian blue ink."

I said, "Oh, yeah, I'm Egyptian." It just came out. That was all I needed to know. That was my bowl.

Bev taught me some things. When I play, I'm trying to take in the energy of it. She said, "First get in relationship. Don't take from it. Get in relationship." I had no consciousness around that. It was key that she spoke to me about that. This bowl is very important. The bowl and I are one and it will be with me doing the work. I didn't even ask the bowl if it wanted to do the work. But she gave me the awareness about the bowl and how to connect with it.

I have my other bowl, which I adore. But this bowl was meant to be; this bowl is very, very important to me. It's significant. My one prerequisite was that the bowl would have to be within my budget. When I said, "I need to get a bowl," my guides said, "Use your credit cards." The credit cards were given to me to help me.

PLUTO'S CAVE, APRIL 6, 2013

After Sky purchases her crystal bowl and we eat lunch, the five of us slated for the "alternate adventure" drive to the parking lot for Pluto's Cave and hike in. The first cave we came to is sad. It has graffiti on the walls and a feeling of having been abused. It isn't a deep cave, rather more like a tunnel with the opening at the other end not far away.

We each find a place to sit that suits us, forming a large circle. Kalia opens a ceremony, beginning by calling in the six directions as she usually does. At some point, Sky begins playing her bowl.

Kalia apparently is seeing a spaceship because she mentions it aloud even though we are meditating by then. With a shock of recognition, I say to myself, "Wait a minute, I know who they are. I *know* them. These are not some strange extraterrestrials from some far away star system. These are your everyday ordinary White Brotherhood members that you can work with at any time. *My friends.*"

After our meditation, we go into the second cave. This one is much deeper and darker. We take pictures of ourselves in the dim light. Those photos show so many orbs present that it looks like it's snowing inside the cave with flakes falling all around us. The energy in this cave is so lovely that we don't want to leave, even though we are due back at the motel for a meeting of our larger group.

UPPER SAND FLAT FAIRY RING, APRIL 6, 2013

While we were at Pluto's Cave, the rest of our group went on a snowshoe hike to Upper Sand Flat.

Later Sage tells me about it.

> We drove to Upper Sand Flat, put on snowshoes, and walked less than half a mile into the woods. We were instructed to find our power spot in a circular clearing. Others walked to the perimeter; I walked to the middle. Some in our group see visions, but usually I don't. For the first time in my life, I saw so much in my imagination. Colors and beings imagined like never before.
>
> We were led on a guided meditation. The concept was that we were to visit Telos. I saw us surrounded

by golden light and transported by elevator deep into the mountain. We were greeted by someone and taken to a space filled with corridors and classrooms. Each of us was clothed in a robe. Mine was crimson.

My ex-husband, who is now deceased, came to me and greeted me with enthusiasm. I saw no faces, I just sensed the beings. I didn't see my ex-husband's face, I just knew his essence.

One room was set aside for science and energy transformation tools. Singing bowls and columns of light were everywhere. My ex-husband was sharing with me the wonder and beauty of our eternal connection. Either on this level or the next one, the perimeter wall was embedded with sparkling gems; and there were columns of white light that glowed.

There was a blue-black lake in the middle with an island in its center. Asian-style wooden bridges, each perhaps ten feet in length, arched from all sides of the lake into the center. In the center was a pagoda-type structure with columns of wood.

The community gathered around the perimeter and sang in harmony in welcome and appreciation of my presence. The singing wasn't a language I understand. It seemed that the whole community was singing, grateful I was there.

Our guide then asked us to leave that space and return to the elevator. My initial thought was that I didn't want to leave, but that thought dissipated as quickly as it came. We returned to the elevator and descended to another level. I no longer wore a robe of crimson; it was now white and gold. Ariel wore ribbons of light woven through her hair. I walked to a labyrinth in the garden. The path was lined with vegetation, herbs and flowers and other nourishment. As I imagined something in red or blue, or another color, it was there.

I walked through the garden to another round central area. I had been all alone and now wondered where my companions were. As I had the thought, they emerged and we merged closer and closer until we became one. We were one unit of being that stretched up taller and taller. We were one. We were then guided back to the elevator once again, and once again I did not want to leave.

On the platform, each of us was given a gift. I was given a small metal key that fit easily into the palm of my hand. I said that I didn't know what it was for and asked for another gift. I was given the gift of Om. Later, as I listened to a recording of crystal bowls, I realized the key was the gift of Om and that I can spend time in meditation and resonate with the bowls.

MIMZY MEETING, APRIL 6, 2013

We arrive back at the motel to meet with our whole group one last time and to share our thoughts and experiences.

Ursa says that by talking together, we create a shared field. Since we are human, we will tend to turn the field into concepts, but at least the concepts will be closer to reality than those uninformed by the field.

After each of us shares his or her thoughts and feelings from the Mimzy event, we drive to the Crystal Room so Bev can give us a crystal bowl activation before we sleep.

CRYSTAL BOWL ACTIVATION, APRIL 6, 2013

The activation is similar to the one that Bev gave Kalia, Marcia, Tess, and me four days ago.

After the activation, many of our group has questions for Bev. At some point, Bev asks me to get the lepidolite bowl from the showroom and bring it to the classroom to show the others how I can play it. I love connecting with it again, but I am very tired and self-conscious trying to play it in front of so many people, so I don't play it well. Bev says, "This bowl and this person are a perfect match between a person and bowl; a perfect reflection of the magnificence of both." I know that Bev sees the magnificence in every person, not just me. Even so, I feel gratified to be spoken of in such a way by a person I so highly respect.

Later Kalia tells me that I was beaming when I played that bowl, and that I should buy it. But I say, "It's like when you go on a date and you have that sparkly feeling of attraction. That doesn't mean it's a marriage. If I have this bowl in my house, I don't want to be neglecting it. It's a responsibility, it's a relationship. If you get a dog from the pound, you can't just put it in your yard and not interact with it."

Kalia asks, "Does that mean you wouldn't play it five minutes a day as part of your meditation?"

I say, "That's what I'm afraid of."

Then Kalia says, "You're right. You shouldn't buy it until you're sure."

DRIVE TIME WITH SKY, APRIL 7, 2013

The next day I drive Sky to the Sacramento International Airport for her flight home. During the three-hour drive we have plenty of time to reflect on both the 2010 and 2013 Mimzy events and their significance.

Sky talks about the changes that we have experienced since the first Mimzy Project three years ago. "This year we all showed up at the motel at about the same time. We were so happy to be together, even with those we didn't know. We were already a field; a field that formed much faster and stronger than three years ago. Three years ago, our field was unstable. This time there wasn't any friction or dissention as before. Three years ago, we yearned for the beginning of unity for ourselves and our planet. Today it is here."

In looking back on my five years of partnering with nature, I say, "In the morning before we went to the pyramid, I was crying as I was reading a passage of the manuscript to you. I was re-experiencing the feeling of being alone and abandoned that I had originally experienced in Shamanic Valley. When it happened, I was sitting on the sofa in my little RV with my computer already on. I grabbed the computer and was typing as the feelings overwhelmed me. As I was typing, I demanded a shift into the reality of being loved and minded every second. That intense experience was all lined up; in retrospect, it had the feeling of being rehearsed.

"You haven't mastered something until you can do it consciously. It can't just be in your dreams or in your imagination. You have to do it in five-senses form. Five years ago when I went out into the desert and asked to be a student of nature, I had to physically go. Now I know that it was rehearsed. The raven went with me. I had to relate to that raven. I had to understand that I was being accompanied. I had to physically say, 'Nature I want to be your student, will you accept me in your School of Nature?'

"After I did this, I wasn't sure that I had connected with anything at all. Had I connected with Nature, had I embarked on some kind of journey? I didn't know. Now, five years later, I know."

The Magic Continues

Getting ready to go is complex. My Nature team has me ask every stone, crystal, and pendent in my house if they want to come with us. A cluster of quartz crystals and the picture jasper stone that sit on the top of my homeopathic remedy cabinet want to go—and they've never wanted to go anywhere before. Also going are the flower essence crystal, the platinum wedding ring that belonged to my mother, a pendant containing some of Skidmore's gold pannings, one of the small crystals that went with me to Peru, and my large crystal that I use for stabilizing flower essences.

I am to wear the serpentine Inca cross pendant that I was given in Peru and the arm beads I got there from the shaman Lorenzo. I am to wear a violet shirt, violet jacket, and green pants. I am to have no caffeine tea for lunch (I was excited enough), but tulsi tea instead. Everything is required to be prepared just so. I put all the stones, crystals, and pendants in a small handbag and walk out the door, ready for my next adventure partnering with Nature.

(. . . to be continued.)

RESOURCES

Recommended Books

Simon Buxton. *The Shamanic Way of the Bee: Ancient Wisdom and Healing Practices of the Bee Masters.* Destiny Books, 2006.

Jorge Luis Delgado with MaryAnn Male, Ph.D. *Andean Awakening: An Inca Guide to Mystical Peru.* Council Oaks Books, 2012.

Masaru Emoto. *The Hidden Messages in Water.* Beyond Words Publishing, 2004.

J.J. Hurtak. *The Seventy-two Sacred Names of the Myriad Expressions of the Living God.* The Academy for Future Science, 1989.

Aurelia Louise Jones. *Revelations of the New Lemuria.* Mount Shasta Light Publishing, 2004.

Machaelle Small Wright. *Behaving as if the God in All Life Mattered.* Perelandra, 1983. Updated and revised 1997.

Machaelle Small Wright. *Co-Creative Science: A Revolution in Science Providing Real Solutions for Today's Health and Environment.* Perelandra, 1997.

Machaelle Small Wright. *The Mount Shasta Mission.* Perelandra, 2005.

Machaelle Wright. *The Perelandra Garden Workbook.* Perelandra, Ltd, 2013.

Flower Essences

More information about the Celestial Gardens flower essences and the aromatherapy/flower essence blends that are described in this book can be found at www.Celestial-Gardens.com.

Genesa Crystals

You can make a small genesa crystal out of paper or a larger one out of metal. Instructions are available by searching online. You can also order premade metal genesa crystals online.

Homeopathy

To contact Maureen Shepard about homeopathy, visit her contact page at www.MaureenShepard.com.

ACKNOWLEDGMENTS

Because of You…

To Machaelle Small Wright: Your book *Co-Creative Science* was the impetus for my journey, and your other books gave me the practical guidance I needed to make progress along the way. Thank you.

To Alison Maslan and the members of the 2011 Pinnacle group: You insisted that I write a book about my experiences with Nature. Your unequivocal assertion that I could do this sustained me when I wasn't sure that I could succeed.

To the members of the 2010 and 2013 Mimzy Projects: Your sense of spiritual adventure and your commitment to healing the planet inspired my own spiritual creativity and gave me a reason to write.

To my writing coach and the members of my writing group: Because of you, I came to believe that I could create writing worth reading.

To all my friends who played a starring role in this story: Thank you for accompanying me on my journey. I've changed your names, but you know who you are.

To Stephanie Gunning: I owe you a special measure of gratitude for your skill, diligence, care, and belief in me. Your editing has been vital to making this a better book.

To my husband: Without your love and support, I could not have written this book. Thank you.

Ascension (of Earth and our solar system) The shift from third to fourth density that we are currently experiencing (see **density**).

Density A vibrational spectrum that our planet and solar system passes through. We are currently experiencing a shift from the spectrum known as third density to the higher vibratory spectrum of fourth density, causing both physical changes in the planet and changes in consciousness of the inhabitants.

Devic realm An intelligent consciousness within nature that creates the designs of specific forms. The Deva of Broccoli is in charge of the design of the broccoli plant. An overlighting deva is one that oversees a large region or a broad area, for example the Overlighting Deva of the United States.

Download (noun) Information received from a source beyond our physical senses, often bypassing the recipient's conscious understanding.

Flower essence A solution created by floating flower petals on water in the sun for a specified time, releasing a healing pattern from the petals into the water. The petals are then removed and a preservative is added. See **mother essence**.

Genesa crystal A spherical energy cleansing device made of four bands in a precise arrangement. The device draws in energy, cleans it, and spirals it back out.

Initiation A spiritual ceremony conferring spiritual knowledge or a higher spiritual state from an initiator to those receiving the initiation.

Mother essence Water infused with a flower essence to which a preservative has been added. The mother essence is not used directly. To prepare the stock concentrate commonly sold, a few drops of the mother essence are added to a small bottle filled with preservative and water.

Ley lines Electromagnetic lines encircling the Earth horizontally and vertically, forming a grid both within the Earth and above the surface. Energy vortices and sacred sites are frequently located on the intersections of ley lines. Information held in the ley lines can be accessed by people on Earth, often unconsciously.

MAP team A team formed to provide medical assistance to an individual composed of the Deva of Healing, Pan, members of the White Brotherhood Medical Unit and the higher self of the individual as detailed in *Map: the Co-creative White Brotherhood Medical Assistance Program* by Machaelle Small Wright.

Nature The order, organization, and life vitality of all form. Nature is an intelligent dynamic that we can connect with, even though this intelligence is not centered in a brain and a sensory system.

Perelandra processes Steps for the cleansing, release, balancing or stabilizing of energy as given in the *Perelandra Garden Workbook, Second Edition* by Machaelle Small Wright.

Violet flame As taught by Saint Germain, the visualization of a violet flame of light in one's heart or around oneself or others.

Wabi-sabi Japanese aesthetic principle that ascribes beauty to objects that are imperfect or incomplete.

About Maureen Shepard

Those who have a compelling story to tell have usually been prepared to tell that story by the way their lives have unfolded. Maureen Shepard is no exception. From her startling childhood spiritual experiences, to her years of training in homeopathy and her unexpected encounter with a raven in the desert, Maureen's experiences have been preparing her to contact the invisible and to translate her resulting adventures into story form. She has also been prepared to convey a practical method for contacting the intelligence in nature that others can use to create their own adventures.

Maureen has been a both small business owner and a librarian who played a role in the automation of libraries. Today she is a certified homeopath and a creator of flower essences. She is also an organic gardener and a beekeeper. She has a husband and two grown sons who are the light of her life.